Superheroes

An Amazing Approach to Helping Children Learn Social/Emotional Insights and Skills

By Steven R. Hitt and
Ellen Greene Stewart

[For Grades 2-6]

Including:

Superhero Play • Superhero Psychology • Walk in a Superhero's Shoes
Create Your Own Superhero

Featuring:

A Curriculum of 70 Lessons with
Highly Motivational, Unforgettable Activities on:
Self-Esteem
Team Building
Bullying
Conflict Resolution
Leadership

youth light inc.

Chapin, SC 29036

Cover Design and Layout by Melody Sandola
Project Editing by Susan Bowman

ISBN
978-1-59850-068-4

Library of Congress Number
2008943808

10 9 8 7 6 5 4 3 2 1
Printed in the United States

Author Biographies

Steven R. Hitt, holds an M.F.A. in Theatre from the University of Florida; and is currently the Managing Director of LaGuardia Performing Arts Center (LPAC) at F. H. LaGuardia Community College in Long Island City, New York. LPAC's mission is to present emerging artists from New York City in all disciplines of the performing arts with a focus on multiculturalism and issues of social justice. Steven has been fortunate to appear on several of the most famous stages in New York City. His longest running role was as Bobby in A Chorus Line; he has danced with American Ballet Theatre at Lincoln Center; sung at Carnegie Hall, and performed at the famed Apollo Theater in Harlem.

In 1991 Steven began using his acting skills with PACT Training; an organization that has harnessed the use of drama to create a simulated experience for people to practice having difficult conversations in emotionally charged situations. He has trained organizations in the U.S, Great Britain, and Canada in all aspects of human dynamics including: Diversity, Customer Service and Leadership.

Steven holds certificates in mediation from the Federal Mediation Conciliation Services, The Institute for the Study of Conflict Transformation and the New York State United Court System where for the past six years he has served as a mediator in civil and family court cases. He has recently continued his education studying Psychology at Goddard College in Vermont. Steven is a local and national member of the Society for Human Resource Management, the Greater New York and National Association for Conflict Resolution, and the Association for Performing Arts Presenters.

Steven currently splits his time between the city of New York and his home in the Catskills where he resides with his life-time partner Tiger, their cat, Mouses, and two lovable dogs, Seiji and Shaw.

Ellen Greene Stewart, MA, ATR-BC, LCAT is a graduate of Goddard College's Psychology and Counseling program. She is a licensed, board certified art therapist, and a certified school counselor. She has been in private practice for the past 8 years. Ms. Stewart has certificates in Disaster Mental Health and Mediation. She has worked with many different populations, including the elderly, patients with dementia, mentally retarded/developmentally delayed adults, at-risk teenagers, families, individuals and school-aged children.

The authors are available as conference speakers and consultants. For more information, contact them at: www.superheroesunmasked.com

Ellen received an innovation award from the National Rural Health Association for her pilot project, an intergenerational art therapy program with nursing home residents. Her previous book, *Kaleidoscope*, is about the uses of art therapy with people who have dementia. She has published numerous articles and reviews in *Activities Director's Quarterly, the American Journal of Alzheimer's Disease,* and *Art Therapy: Journal of the American Art Therapy Association.*

Ellen is particularly interested in rural psychology and rural mental health issues, systems theory, as well as art therapy with survivors of breast cancer. She is working on a series of articles to be included in a book addressing the issues of rural mental health. For the past seven years, Ellen has worked with troubled and traumatized children within rural schools and in private practice, and has been the Site Director for an after school enrichment program. She also teaches writing classes using art to enhance the creative process.

A breast cancer survivor, Ellen lives in the northern Catskill Mountains with her husband and daughter, a sheepdog named Fudgie, an angora rabbit named Snickers, a dwarf rabbit named Marley, Ali and Brownie the guinea pigs and a small fruit grove.

Dedications

Ellen Stewart: This book is dedicated to Bob and Lacey Peace Stewart whose love and support sustain me.

Steven Hitt: This book is dedicated to Tiger for his love and support.

Acknowledgements

As in any endeavor, there are so many family members, colleagues, and friends who gave their support, knowledge and enthusiasm along the way.
Among them are:

Dr. Maxine Borowsky Junge, mentor, colleague and friend extraordinaire

Alice Fiske, Tonya Liberatore, Joan Riordan, Amy Royal and Barbara Spanhake of

Roxbury Central School, Roxbury, NY

Tom O'Brien, Superintendent, Roxbury Central School

Frank Canavan and Joyce St. George, friends and mentors
The acronym S.U.P.E.R. used in this book is based on a conflict resolution model called S.A.F.E developed by and used with the permission of Joyce St. George and PACT Training.

Our friend Kent Brown of PACT Training Inc.

Kris Kaschak, Betsy Kenney, and Loretta McCormick of the Creating Rural Opportunities Partnership (CROP) program for after school enrichment, whose support has always been invaluable

The A. Lindsay and Olive B. O'Connor Foundation, Hobart, New York

Nancy Millen and Gary Robeson of Margaretville Central School, Margaretville, NY

Ben Berliner, John Bonhotal, Sally Becker, Jo Boring, and the Elementary Teachers of South Kortright Central School, South Kortright, NY.

Laurie Greene

Bethany Lyttle and Phil Weinberg

Mimi Sandeen, Editor

Susan Baker and Karen Grace of Union Institute and University

Table of Contents

Goals for Superhero Emotional Intelligence Curriculum:

· Emotional self-awareness and identification of emotions
· Increased self-esteem
· Better frustration tolerance
· Identifying and handling conflict
· Better anger management skills
· Fewer classroom and playground disputes
· Decline in frequency of bullying
· Improvement in handling stress and setbacks
· Decreased loneliness, more inclusion
· Increased empathy for others
· Improved listening skills
· Building skills to identify emotions in others
· More self-control, less impulsiveness
· Clearer expression of emotions
· Increased helpfulness
· Increased peer/group involvement/teambuilding
· Better at handling conflicts peacefully
· Impulse control
· Being able to resist negative situations
· Minimize self-blame, enhance self-reflection
· To help children feel better supported
· Increased empathy and compassion for others
· Teach children a vocabulary of emotional terms
· Enable children to form positive friendships
· Normalize some emotions
· Help create a sense of emotional safety in the classroom
· Educate students about heroes in their community
· Educate students about villains and their role in conflict
· Educate children about problem solving methods
· Teach the difference between tattling and asking for help

Introduction

We wrote this book to create the text we wish had been available when we were young and struggling emotionally. Each of us separately had a significant emotional "event" around age twelve. Perhaps if an emotional literacy curriculum were used in those days, the "events" would have been less traumatic to our lives. But for both of us, through the hard work of therapy, the emotional crisis eventually became a turning point in our lives; it was the beginning of learning about our emotional selves. That turning point was a point of no return. Never again would we be emotionally unequipped. We separately and then together pledged to find a way to help all children increase their emotional intelligence skills.

This book is for elementary school students, their teachers, parents, counselors, scout leaders and school administrators. We deliberately use the Multiple Intelligences as defined by Gardner (1993), recognizing that everyone learns differently. Therefore, we have used a variety of intelligences including kinesthetic methods, musical, verbal, linguistic, visual and spatial. Effective learning takes place when all parts of the brain are engaged.

Children emulate the adults they spend the most time with: parents and teachers and other leaders. It is thus important for faculty and staff to participate along with children whenever possible to provide a level of comfort for those who are hesitant as well as to increase the level of trust.
In addition to what is covered in the program, students should be encouraged to suggest other related topics to cover.

How to Use This Book

The overriding goals of the 70 activities in this book were designed to help children become emotionally aware of themselves and others. We help them examine their behavior, look at ways they may be contributing to conflict, and learn tools for the peaceful resolution of conflict.

We use superheroes as role models and villains as a way of viewing "negative behavior" once removed from ourselves. Tolerance, clear communication, emotional expression, emotional awareness, cooperation, teambuilding, leadership and conflict resolution are the skills we hope this program will clarify for all participants.

We begin by talking about commercial superheroes and villains, and then encourage each student to create his/her own superhero and villain, complete with super powers. By using their imaginations, children become aware of their own "superpowers" or strengths. This awareness leads to the understanding of other emotions, ways of solving problems, conflicts, and using their new found "superpowers" for proactively building team member and leadership skills.

Don't try to fit a square peg into a round hole. The authors want to emphasize that this program is student-centered and that the order of these exercises may not fit every group all the time. This is a guide for what we believe is the best approach. If you see that the next exercise isn't appropriate, feel free to skip to the next exercise or look in section 7 for additional exercises that might fit better.

Although we have indicated the approximate length of each exercise, we suggest for optimal results that you map out an afternoon or a 2-hour block of time in which to complete one entire lesson. Perhaps each Friday afternoon would work well. If you are not able to block out that large an amount of time, each exercise can be done in the approximate time indicated.

Lastly, we can't emphasize enough that the process of children learning to understand themselves and others is always more important than the products produced. In other words, the journey is more important than the destination.

Section 1: Why Emotional Intelligence?

What exactly is emotional intelligence? And a related question: why is it so important to teach emotional intelligence to children? With so much crammed into our academic days, where can we find the time to teach these skills? What are the long-term ramifications of teaching emotional intelligence? Why are we seeing an increase in violent behaviors in schools across the country?

Emotional intelligence is an ability or capacity to perceive, understand, assess, and manage the emotions of one's self, of others, and of oneself within groups. Teaching ways to identify and describe emotions is the first step for young children toward developing emotional intelligence. Until a child can name what he or she is feeling, it is all guesswork.

Emotionally intelligent individuals have a distinct advantage in life. Most students today are not taught these people-reading skills anywhere else in their lives. It is a set of skills that is the key to successful interpersonal relationships and problem solving.

People with emotional intelligence are not only astute about their own feelings, but they are very perceptive in reading the feelings of others. They are usually more prone to seeing the cup half full, and helping others to see it that way as well. They are more empathetic, better listeners, more insightful about the motivations of others, more socially adept, maintain better relationships with others and are better able to solve conflicts to everyone's advantage peacefully.

Emotional intelligence sets the stage for success in life, and we can help our students learn this often ignored subject. Among the benefits of teaching emotional intelligence are improved academic performance, greater sense of self-confidence, increased social and conflict resolution skills and less violence. Through this type of learning, we can create better decision makers, empathizers and leaders of a more peaceful world. We can enable our students to become agents of positive change using whatever unique traits he or she possesses.

Being a relatively new area in psychology, the definition of emotional intelligence is still in a state of flux. There are four main skills inherent in Emotional Intelligence. Goleman (2005) defines them as:

- Self-Awareness – the ability to observe oneself, recognize feelings, build a vocabulary for them and know the relationship between thoughts, feelings and reactions.
- Self-Management or managing feelings – monitoring "self-talk." Accepting one's thoughts, feelings, capabilities, imperfections in the present moment.
- Social Awareness – awareness of the dynamics of group interactions and behavior.
- Relationship Awareness – an awareness of the mechanics of relationships, of what makes them special, successful, or dysfunctional.

Goleman adds that traditional IQ tests tap the cortical part of the brain which controls intellect. The emotional brain, however, controls every emotion we experience, from rage to deep love, and is molded largely by experiences and feelings. Traditional IQ tests miss emotional intelligence completely.

There is a physiological basis for the inability to think straight when we're emotionally upset. Anxiety and depression have been proven to adversely affect intellect, and when prolonged can change brainwave patterns and brain chemistry. Altered brainwave patterns can carve deficits in a child's academic abilities by making it difficult for them to learn. Good moods have been proven to enhance flexibility and creativity of thought, which are among the key skills needed to solve a complex problem. Most behavior issues with children occur because of unmet needs. Whether hungry or tired, in need of a different form of instruction, a lack of nurturing at home or being bullied by peers; any one of these issues is enough to cause a child to seek attention, even negative attention. Consider how so many of our young people are living lives full of stress, neglect, economic depravity and sometimes violence.

It is critical, then, to provide children, particularly young children, with the vocabulary of emotions so that they can begin to express themselves clearly and appropriately. So many children are happy, sad, or mad, and they do not have the language to apply those or other feelings that lie in between. All adults who work with children can teach them these feeling descriptors directly as vocabulary words, or indirectly through monitoring play, conversation, and through special programs such as this one.

In order for students to successfully learn emotional intelligence, they must first feel they are in a safe and nurturing place. Try having a discussion with your students about what will make them feel physically and emotionally safe. Unconditional acceptance and a non-judgmental stance are the tools therapists use to foster a safe, nurturing relationship with a child.

Promoting and positively reinforcing emotional intelligence throughout the day will strengthen these feeling words and activities. Photos of people with a variety of expressions can be displayed around the room, or throughout the building. Facilitators can acknowledge their own feelings and praise those who express their feelings succinctly. A great many of the national and state curriculum standards can be taught through or linked to this program.

Section 2: Why Superheroes?

The children of today will be the leaders of tomorrow. Let's give them the tools they need in order to make a sure positive impact on this crazy world of ours. Let's insure that the voice of our future leaders is emotionally intelligent, and that those leaders are agents of positive change.

A Brief History of Superheroes

Mythic heroes have existed since man first began communicating. Superheroes defy aging, stagnation and death. They give rise to our hopes and dreams, and they restore our faith that good can triumph over evil. Superheroes provide us with a safe cathartic vehicle through which we can release anger, aggression, anxiety and other emotions. When locked inside ourselves, these emotions become toxic.

The earliest forms of superheroes were the Greek and Roman myths. The Bible provides us with a wealth of sages, and heroes, such as David, Moses, Abraham, and others who are thought to have superpowers. Psychologist Rollo May (1991) believed that myth can be either regressive, expressing archetypal struggles between our instinctual forces, or progressive, revealing new insights and solutions. Joseph Campbell (1988) on the other hand, believed dreams or fantasies are personal myths, whereas myths outside of us are collective dreams and fantasies. This goes along with psychologist C.G. Jung's (1993) idea of the collective unconscious, that a collection of memories and types of characters called archetypes, are assumed to be shared by mankind.

What is Superhero Play?

We believe that superhero or fantasy play is an essential developmental steppingstone. It is also a natural phenomenon. We spend a great deal of our waking hours daydreaming. We dream at night, and escape into the fantasy world when we are under stress, whether through books, movies or plays.

For the purposes of this book, we have defined superhero play in a very broad sense. It is any form of play that focuses on children's fantasies of good vs. evil, safe vs. dangerous, powerful vs. powerlessness, bravery vs. cowardice, inclusion vs. exclusion, right vs. wrong, fair vs. unfair, and life vs. death. This goes along with Erickson's (1980) competing drives of dependence vs. independence, initiative vs. guilt, which addresses a sense of purpose; and industry vs. inferiority, which addresses a sense of competence in school aged children. In addition, superhero play can help children understand issues of power and control, and allow them an opportunity to feel empowered in a world where adults hold all of the power.

Russian psychologist Lev Vygotsky (in Rubin, 2007) believed that in play, children act above their age and normal behavior. By engaging in superhero play in a broad sense, children are able to balance the competing demands placed on them and come to understand them. Children also test their physical limits through play.

The cast of characters in such a make-believe world include kings, queens and other royalty; witches and werewolves; fairies and monsters; stepmothers and siblings; and many more. Many of these personalities have transformative abilities, such as the frog that turns into a prince, the man who turns into a werewolf, and the jester who performs magic tricks.

According to Vivian Gussin Paley (2004), fantasy play is, "the glue that binds together all other pursuits, including the early teaching of reading and writing skills." Paley acknowledges that fewer and fewer adults who work with young children are willing to "risk" allowing fantasy play, yet fantasy play is the "natural style and substance of early childhood."

What Are the Benefits of Superhero Play?

Ultimately, superhero play can teach children how to settle conflicts in a non- violent way, and how to act with compassion toward others who need help. According to Hoffman (2004), "This approach can show children how to use power wisely, understand the difference between real violence and pretend violence, settle conflicts without hurting anyone, and act with compassion when others need help… They are learning what people do to feel powerful and how people who have power use it. They are exploring how to handle their fears and desires. While we can shield them for a short time from those who abuse their authority, sooner or later they will confront violence, racism, and other corruptions of power, both in the media and in the real world. Superhero play is a way children say to us, 'I want to know more about these things. I want to know what I should do about them. What can you teach me?' When we ban the play, we are telling children that their questions scare us."

Superhero play may be a productive means to counter the negative effects of contemporary society on childhood. These include consumerism, media bombardment, strained family ties, poverty, spending too much time using electronic devices, and over-stimulation. Children in this day and age, more than ever are pushed to perform, conform, adapt and grow up quickly. Heroes are distinct from parents, teachers, and other significant adults, and can provide struggling children with hope.

For young children, *Where the Wild Things Are,* by Maurice Sendak (1963) is a wonderful example of this. In this story, Max, a young boy, tries on a wolf suit, which causes him to act wild like a wolf. He is sent to his room without dinner. While lying in bed, he dreams of an encounter on a desert island with Wild Things. He is able to stop them from harming him by staring at them without blinking. They appoint him king of the Wild Things. By trying on a persona and finding himself a superpower, Max learns to confront his demons.

On the neuropsychological level, superhero play is especially valuable to the vast numbers of children who have experienced trauma, abandonment, harsh punishment, or domestic violence. Although these severe stresses change brain chemistry, scientists have realized that the brain has an amazing amount of plasticity, and can be taught to react in new ways. Superhero play appeals to the limbic system which controls facial expressions, tone of voice, body language and some aspects of movement, because of the strong visual and emotional affects.

One important part of the attraction children (and adults) have to superheroes is that many of them have secret identities or alter egos. According to Rubin (2007), "Children can use the vehicle of secret identity in two ways: either to cloak their weaknesses psychologically or to imagine (future) transformation into more powerful figures…Regardless of the adequacy or inadequacy of the foster parenting of the orphaned, neglected, or abandoned superheroes, the superhero maintains hope that someday he or she will be restored to a family of truly loving and understanding parents."

Implementing Superhero Play

By the time children reach Kindergarten, they should be aware of the difference between reality and fantasy in play. Trying on some of these make-believe roles is part of healthy play. Many adults have concerns about the physical safety of such play, the reliance on violence to solve problems. We advocate setting firm, clear safety limits prior to the start of the program. Rules should be made as a group activity, so children understand how they can get what they need in acceptable ways. If dolls, stuffed animals or puppets are used, the students can even be encouraged to make rules based on the imagined opinions of these characters.

Rules for this program should include the consequences for breaking a rule, where these activities will take place, at what designated time, and how to resolve conflicts without resorting to violence. Leaders of these activities can redirect inappropriate behavior based on the healthy impulses of those involved in the play scenario. Since children engrossed in this type of imaginative play don't always remember the rules, we recommend periodic pauses in play to review the rules, especially with younger students.

The elements of a story include strong characters that kids can identify with. There must be a conflict, fear, or event that the characters must solve or face. Children in higher grades can add more complicated elements, such as a more thorough setting of the scene, more characters, more twists and turns in the plot. If students are proposing a story that involves violence, ask the whole class if they approve of this method of solving the problem, and if there are alternate means of solving it. According to Hoffman (2004), "I have found that they will accept stories that don't depend on killing evil monsters with lethal weapons when there is an exciting story available that uses bravery and clever thinking to solve the problem."

Regarding violence as a choice, and the anger that accompanies violence, when a child learns to recognize that what appears to be anger in a peer could really be fear or hurt, they can better create positive outcomes to conflict. A large part of emotional literacy is learning to identify feelings and the words and body language used to describe those feelings. Imaginary monsters are most often symbols that represent children's fear, worry, and anger.

According to Winner (1982), the main themes in early stories were found to be violent ones. Preschool children frequently tell stories about danger and disaster in which characters fall down and die, or get devoured by monsters. But children also protect themselves against disaster. For example, bad things usually happen to other people in their stories, but not to the storytellers themselves. Sometimes the storyteller or one of the characters "undoes" the disaster at the end of the story. Common adult concerns related to superhero play include fears that differences are threatening, that conflicts must always be won, that aggression always works, and that weapons lead to victory.

If we as adults educate children and then give them a chance to try to solve their own problems, they will learn, even if their solution was unsuccessful. In other words, they can try various solutions in this program while being carefully guided by adult facilitators.

In her book, Invented Worlds (1982), Ellen Winner classified a developmental stage of literary development. By age five, children can construct coherent stories with a beginning, middle, and end. The events of the story are causally connected, and they revolve around a central conflict that the main character must confront. These stories are clearly extracted from the world of reality, and the boundary between the constructed and the given world is no longer violated.

Genres of Children's Stories

There are many genres of children's stories: fairy tales, simple good/bad monster stories, and nursery rhymes in which the structure, rhythm and rhyme are of the utmost importance. Storytelling allows children to express their fears, concerns, and nightmares in order to safely explore these feelings.

The hero folktales of many cultures exhibit four types of content (Maranda and Maranda, 1971). In the first type, one power overwhelms another, and the minor power makes no attempt at response. In the second, one power overwhelms another, and the minor power attempts a response but fails. In the third type, one power overwhelms another, who then nullifies the threat. And in the fourth, one power overwhelms another, who nullifies the threat, and the original circumstances are substantially transformed. Although hero tales of all four types exist, in cultures with little belief in control over fate, the fourth kind is seldom found.

Applying this classification to the stories of children between the ages of five and ten revealed a progression in complexity from level one to level four. In a typical level one story, the main character is overcome by a powerful, evil figure, shows little or no response. In a level two story, the main character responds to the threat not enough to do away with the threat. Even though the hero may escape, there is no guarantee that the danger won't return. The hero may escape from the villain, but the villain is still in the picture. At level four, the hero not only slays the villain but also marries the princess and they live together happily ever after.

IIn the chart below, various types of developmental theories are mapped out for comparison. Piaget (1996) and Erickson (1980) represent theories from developmental psychologists, while Lowenfeld's (1987) developmental stages refer to the stages of artistic development. Winner (1980) delineates stages of literary development in stories children write.

Piaget Developmental	**Erikson Dvelopmental**	**Winner LIterary**	**Lowenfeld Artistic**
Birth – 2 yrs. Sensorimotor	Trust vs. Mistrust		
2-7 years – preoperational thinking	Autonomy vs. Shame and Doubt	By age 5, stories have beginning, middle and end. Main character overcome by evil	2-4 yrs. Scribbling stage random marks
7-11 years – concrete stage	Initiative vs. Guilt Industry vs. inferiority	Main character responds to threat, but danger may not be over	Age 4-7 pre-schematic – 1st representational attempts
11 years and up formal operations	Identity vs. Role Confusion	Threat is nullified Stage 4- hero marries princess, peace prevails	Age 7-9 Schematic stage Development of forms

Section 3: Superheroes: Not just people in tights

Four Superheroes demonstrate how ordinary people can overcome adversity to fight against evil.

The Case of Batman™

As a young boy, Bruce Wayne witnessed the brutal murder of both of his parents. His vow to fight crime is a compensatory wish. Is it significant that we never see Batman's™ eyes since there is always a mask over them? Is he literally covering his eyes as a response to the horrific crime he witnessed as a youth? Batman™uses learning in order to better himself, by studying science and athletic training. He has figured out how to use the Judeo-Christian work ethic and disciplined accumulation of knowledge to overcome adversity. Batman™ is tortured by survivor's guilt, and his symptoms and recovery from trauma follow the bulk of psychological literature on trauma.

Batman's™ story demonstrates Erikson's (1968), developmental conflict of industry vs. inferiority. These stages, which are parallel in age to Freud's (oral, anal, phallic, latency), are external and relate to the world at large, whereas Freud's stages relate to the individual him/herself. In order to help children master this psychosocial stage of development, we must find ways to help them feel worthwhile, competent, included and empowered.

It is wonderful to watch a school aged child realize that Batman™ gets angry just like the child does, and realize that personal tragedy can be transformed into appropriate aggression, assertiveness, and that one can choose to become a transformative agent in the world, pulling positive lessons from negative experiences. We all have the need for an outlet for venting anger appropriately. So many children have been taught that anger is "bad". In fact, anger can motivate and energize and push through fears and obstacles.

The Case of the Incredible Hulk™

According to Rubin (2007):

The legend of the Incredible Hulk™ illustrates that mild-mannered Bruce Banner had a problem from the beginning. Originating from the disconnection from others and the absence of healthy relationships in childhood, Bruce never learned to effectively express his emotions. Like many toxic substances or traumatic experiences, the gamma rays that Bruce Banner was exposed to merely exacerbated his already-present inability to express emotions unless provoked to the point of rage. Although academically and intellectually gifted, Bruce lacked the capacity to differentiate anger from other emotions, (p. 90).

There are four types of anger present in the Incredible Hulk Syndrome (Potter-Efron and Potter-Efron, 1995). Some are found in Bruce Banner, the human; the others are found in the Hulk™ himself.

- *Suppressed anger, in which the real feeling is denied or minimized and other emotions like anxiety or guilt are substituted.
- *Explosive anger, which is suppressed anger over a prolonged period of time that results in exaggerated and sometimes destructive output of rage.
- *Chronic anger, a personality style that holds onto anger for extended periods of time, which results in somatic complaints and ailments.
- *Healthy anger – the use of anger to signal a problem, rather than solve the problem.

The Hulk™ only comes out when someone is in danger. He is highly aware of the difference between random destruction and self-protection.

Wonder Woman™

Wonder Woman™ was created in 1941 in response to the need for a female superhero/heroine. Created by Harvard psychologist William Moulton Marston, the same person who invented the systolic blood pressure test and the lie detector, Wonder Woman comes out of the Greek mythological tradition of an all-female tribe of Amazons. Wonder Woman has all the strength of Superman plus all the allure of a gorgeous woman who is also a good person. Her Lasso of Truth gives her the ability to discern the truth from a lie, much like the lie detector invented by her creator. In addition to her lasso, Wonder Woman wears two bullet-deflecting bracelets and has an invisible plane.*

Mighty Mouse™

Mighty Mouse is an anthropomorphic mouse whose powers include super strength, hand to hand combat ability and, in some versions, the ability to fly and X-ray vision. He uses his superpowers to battle bullying cats in order to protect the other mice. For the purpose of this book, it's important to note that superheroes can come in the most unlikely of forms, and this allows students to expand their horizons beyond the forms of human male and female superheroes.

All Superheroes Need Villains

A superhero is nothing without a villain. Like superheroes, villains are smart, highly motivated, often have traumatic origins, and are powerful in their costumes. According to Fingeroth (2004) villains can be seen as having more clearly defined values than those of heroes. They are compelled to change the world. That compulsion may stem from a need for revenge or a thirst for power. A "good villain" will bring chaos to an orderly world and will not be persuaded to act otherwise. Does this ensuing chaos sound familiar in terms of some current political and religious conflicts, as well as some world-changing conflicts throughout history?

The fictional representation of these conflicts is one of the major appeals of superhero fiction. We enjoy seeing conflicts and crises similar to our own acted out by characters in capes with superpowers. Seeing the ease with which superheroes solve problems makes us feel that our issues are more manageable and that there are actual solutions to serious problems – possibly even solutions without negative consequences. When a superhero solves a problem, it usually stays solved. The super villain, however, is still on the prowl.

Reynolds (1992) sees superheroes as reactive, not out to change the world except to rid it of evil. The villains, on the other hand, are seen as very proactive and interested in changing the world, but for his/her own benefit. He believes, "In the Jungian sense, the epic battles between superheroes and super villains represent the battles within each of us."

The villain represents the dark side of the hero, and personifies an idea or goal so strong it would be hard to rid the world of it. And we utilize the psychological concept of projection with villains – we dislike in others exactly what we dislike in ourselves.

Section 4: Creating the Superheroes

Introduction: This is the introduction to the program, including a focus on safety, confidentiality (what happens in the room stays in the room) and the establishment of personal and group goals during the program. Let students know that in addition to what is covered in the program, you can cover other issues if they have suggestions.

A suggestion box can be decorated and displayed prominently, so that suggestions are offered confidentially. Superhero wrapping paper works well for this. Faculty and staff are encouraged to participate whenever possible to create an atmosphere of equality and to discourage hesitancy.

This is a good time to engage children in extra helping roles. Ideas for this phase include older students reading to younger students, students helping clean a classroom together, working on a project that benefits the whole school such as gardening or composting, collecting magazines or cans and bottles for recycling, etc. These activities enable children to experience feeling good about themselves individually and collectively as part of a group with a common goal.

To foster a high level of safety and nurturance for all students, the facilitator will introduce and explain important ground rules for participation.

- Everyone is expected to participate. If an exercise or discussion becomes too emotionally painful for a student, she/he can be allowed to pass.
- Everyone's ideas are important.
- No ideas are silly.
- It's ok to add to someone else's idea.
- Everyone will help one another.
- Everyone will be a good listener.
- Everyone will honor each other's differences
- Everyone will refrain from making fun of or criticizing another's ideas or actions.
- Those making negative comments will be encouraged to make two positive comments.
- Everyone will look out for everyone else's safety as well as their own.
- Only one person speaks at a time.
- Participants may ask for clarification.
- We feel it important at this point to include a note about resistance. Resistance can be a healthy response when asking children to learn about themselves. We urge parents, teachers, counselors and facilitators to work with the resistance, and try to help the child identify its source. Uncovering the source of that resistance can be a springboard to growth.

A Word of Caution: before beginning this or any program having to do with human emotions, be sure someone is available to students, such as a teacher, counselor, social worker, or other leader who can address any powerful feelings that come up during the exercises.

Lesson 1

Superheroes, Self-Awareness, & Self-Esteem

Time: 30 minutes

Objective: To establish the foundation of the program.

Introduction: We're going to spend the next few weeks discussing superheroes.

- Who can tell me what a superhero is? *(Superman™, strong person, someone with superpowers, etc.)* The definition of a superhero is someone who uses an extraordinary power or gift to perform extraordinary random acts of kindness. (This is our definition, but you can adapt it as you see fit).
- Who is your favorite superhero or heroine? (Batman™, Batgirl™, Wonder Woman™, Superman™, Spiderman™, The Incredibles™, etc.). The authors have provided access to the following web site so that the program can be better linked with issues of diversity: www.internationalhero.co.uk.* We do not pretend to be experts on superheroes. We use them as a way to discuss behaviors affecting children.
- What superpowers does s/he possess? (Flying, spinning webs, Bat mobile, jet, etc).
- What does the superhero do with his/her powers? (Fight bad people, combat evil, etc.)
- Do superheroes have weaknesses? (Yes). Such as? (Kryptonite, Anger, etc.)
- Who are some of the bad people they fight? (Lex Luther, Joker, Penguin, Catwoman, The Ice Man, etc.)
- Do the bad people have superpowers? (some do). Name them. (The ability to fly, x-ray vision, ice-making, etc.)
- What makes them "bad people"? (They hurt others, rob banks, cause chaos, steal puppies, etc.)
- What is a superhero?
- What makes them special?
- What goals do you think they have?
- What do they have in common?
- Can you name any other superheroes?
- What powers do they have?
- How do they use their powers?
- Do they have enemies?
- Does one person always win? Why?

* As of the time this book went to press, this website was fully operational.

Activity 1.1 Let's Be Reporters

Objective: To develop listening skills and an understanding of superheroes through interviewing.

Time: 45 minutes

Introduction: Very soon we will be creating our own superhero and giving them a special superpower. Think for a minute about what kind of superhero you want to create. Close your eyes if you want and put your head down to think about the following questions:

- What is their favorite food?
- What do they like to play?
- Do they have parents and siblings?
- Do they have pets?
- How do they spend their time when they're not needed as superheroes?
- Do the have special powers when they're not needed as superheroes?
- Who are their friends?
- Do they wear a costume?
- What else can you tell us about your favorite superhero?

Directions: Superman™ was Clark Kent during the day. Clark Kent worked with Lois Lane at the Daily Planet newspaper. They were both reporters.

Divide the class into pairs. One person will act as the reporter and interview the other about favorite superheroes. After a few minutes students will switch roles with their partner. At the end of the interviews, the reporter will explain to the class details about the lives of their partner's favorite superheroes. For younger grades, facilitators can model interviewing techniques for students, and each student can report on their own favorite superhero.

When all the groups have finished, the reporters respond to the class. Facilitators will want to write notes on the board so the class can compare information on their favorite superheroes for a concluding discussion.

Follow Up:

- How did it feel to be the reporter? Good? Scary?
- Did you report the information to the class accurately?
- Was the reporter accurate in reporting your information?
- What needs to be clarified?
- How did it feel to be interviewed as the superhero?

Activity 1.2 Creating Super Secret Information Journals

Approximate Time: 20 minutes

Objective: To incorporate English Language Skills and track progress of the program.

Introduction: We are going to create journals now to keep track of our superhero adventures. All your ideas, super secrets and other information will be kept in this journal. You may decorate your journal with any of the supplies here, and we will use it throughout this program.

Materials: letter-size paper, construction paper for the journal pages or wrapping paper for cover, markers, crayons and other decorating materials, stapler. Journals can be made in 8 ½ x 11 format, or folded in half.

Directions: Participants are provided with materials for journal making, along with a discussion of the joys and benefits of journaling. These journals are to be used at the end of each session or as homework for students to record their feelings about each day's session. They are not to be graded but, merely used as a self-reflective tool to reinforce what is learned in each session and to identify how well a student understands the concepts presented.

Activity 2.1: Superheroes, Villains and Everything In Between

This exercise utilizes the information presented by the reporters from Lesson 1.

Approximate Time: 15 minutes

Objectives: To review previous session and to visualize the differences and similarities between superheroes, super villains and all people.

Materials: Venn diagram, pens, pencils, crayons.

Directions:

- Label the top left circle to say Superheroes, and label the top of the right circle to read Villains.
- Write the characteristics of each under the headings, and in the center write the traits that are common to both. For example:
    - Do they both have superpowers?
    - Are they both very determined people?
    - Do they follow what they believe in?
    - Are there more similarities or differences between them?

Venn Diagram

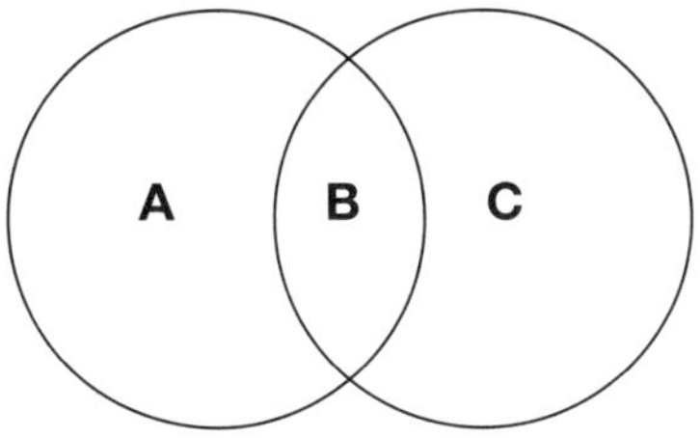

Activity 2.2: Creating your Superhero

Approximate Time: 45 minutes

Objective: To encourage imaginative and creative thinking, and provide opportunities for self-expression.

Introduction:

- Encourage each student to think about what they will name their superhero, how it will look, and act, and what special superpower it will have.
- Each superhero should have a vulnerability or weakness in addition to a superpower. (Example: Superman™ and Kryptonite™)

Each student will draw, present and explain their superhero for the class. The superheroes will be hung on the wall or bulletin board for the next few weeks. We will call it our "Hall of Heroes." Remember, your superhero can only have one superpower and must have one vulnerability or weakness.

Materials: Outline of a human form, paint, glitter, yarn, sequins, buttons, fabric scraps, crepe or tissue paper and anything else that is readily available and would enhance the look of a superhero.

Directions:

- Review the superhero words, the list of superheroes in our community and review qualities of commercial superheroes.
- Distribute the non-gendered human outline on the next page and ask students to create their own superhero.
- Encourage them to think about whether their superhero will be a boy or a girl, what color hair and eyes s/he will have, what their costume will look like, what his/her superpower will be, etc.
- Review students' superheroes, and reiterate that they use their power for good causes.
- Discuss the other characters or alter egos such as Clark Kent for Superman, Bruce Wayne for Batman, etc. This side of the superhero leads an everyday life and still acts for the good of others.
- Emphasize that superpowers are a last resort, to be used when all else fails. Now you have a superpower in your superhero character to call on when you need it.

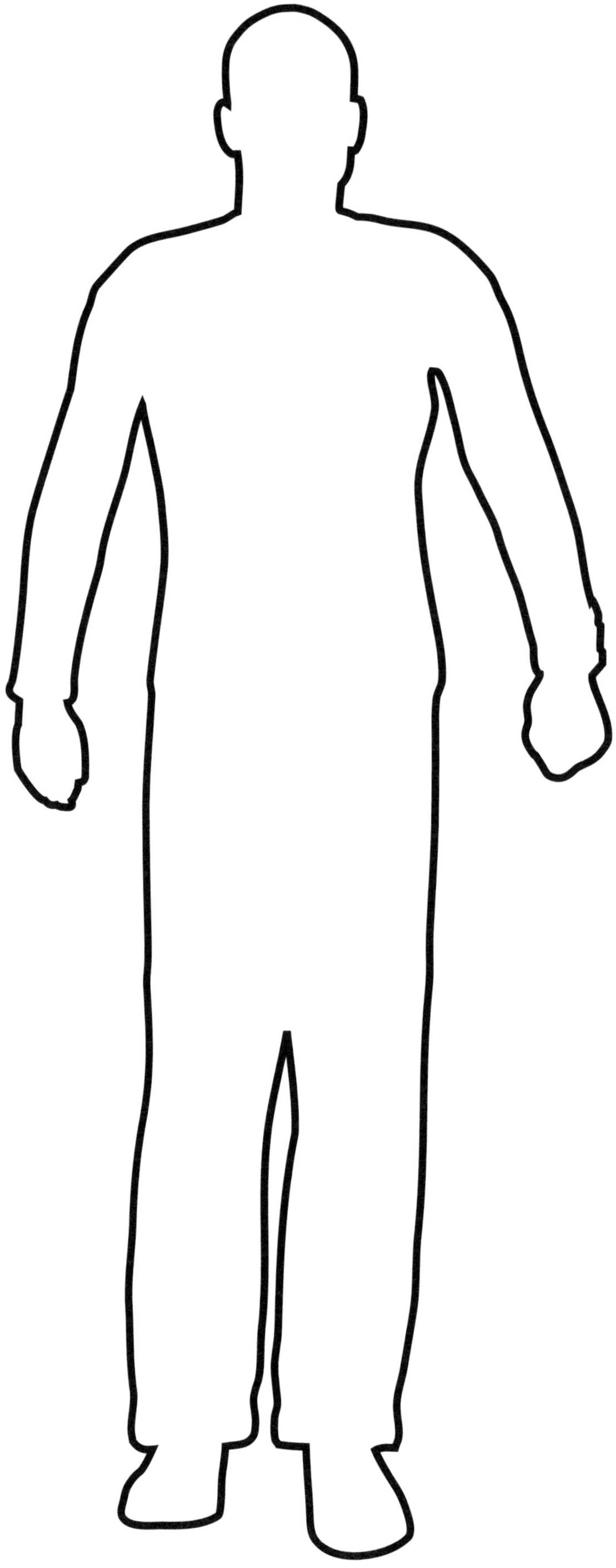

Activity 2.3: Listening is a Superpower

Approximate Time: 30 minutes

Objective: To introduce listening as a tool for facilitating good interpersonal relationships.

Discussion: Listening is an important skill in helping children develop emotional literacy. There are different types of listening, each of which has their place in empowering students. According to Adler & Towne (1996), active listening, sometimes referred to as reflective listening is, "restating a speaker's thoughts and feelings in the listener's own words." Active listening involves eye contact and body language that shows the speaker you are really listening.

One type of active listening is reflective listening. This is a skill that involves careful listening and then summarizing what was said back to the speaker. This technique helps ensure that communication is clear and totally understood.

Understand what the other person is trying to say. If you say, "I'd like to understand your idea, could you explain it to me?" the other person becomes aware that what they have to say is important to you. Share your side in a similar way. If you don't understand their point of view, ask them to explain it again in a different way. Use reflective listening or summarize until both parties are clear as to what the disagreement is about. Some ways to do that are, "What I heard you say is…", or "You feel…."

Let's practice reflective listening superpowers. (Model reflective listening with a student). After each person in the class speaks about a conflict, the person to their right summarizes what was said to the satisfaction of the original speaker.

Lesson 3

Activity 3.1: Superheroes Commit Random Acts of Kindness

Time: 30 minutes

Objective: To understand heroic actions in everyday terms.

Introduction: Random acts of kindness are small things we can do for each other to help us feel happy and cared about. Often, you don't ever find out who did a random act of kindness for you. Superheroes do random acts of kindness all the time. They make sure people cross the street safely, rescue cats from trees, and keep villains from hurting people. Your parents, teachers, significant adults and friends do random acts of kindness for you all the time. It could be that someone in your family bought your favorite food at the grocery store. Or it could be that someone left a special snack in your desk. Maybe someone gave you an extra hug today. Maybe your friends will invite you to join them for something special. What if your teacher gave you some extra time at recess one day?

- How do you feel when someone does a random act of kindness for you?
- How do you feel when you do a random act of kindness for someone else?
- What are some examples of random acts of kindness?
- Are there people in your community who commit random acts of kindness?
- Who are they?

Materials: paper, pencils.

Directions:
- We are going to break into groups of 3.
- Each group is going to write a list of random acts of kindness we can do for our school and community.
- When you are all finished, we will share your ideas and vote on which one we will perform as a group.

Activity 3.2: Villains and the Quest for Chaos

Time: 20 minutes

Objective: Introduce children to the dark side of life to understand the nature of conflict.

Discussion: The villain represents the dark side of the hero, and personifies an idea or goal so strong it would be hard to rid the world of it. Discuss the following:

- Villains are evil characters who do bad things in order to better themselves. What famous villains can you name and describe? (Darth Vader™, Ice Man™, Joker™, Penguin™, Voldemort™, etc.)
- When might your superhero need to use their power? (When they are attacked).
- What do you think you would call your superheroes' arch nemesis or villain?
- What does s/he look like? What is the color of their hair, eyes, and skin? Are they tall or short, chubby, skinny or medium in build?
- What powers do they have?
- How do they use their powers?
- Are they 100% evil, or do they have some good qualities?

Activity 3.3: Creating your Super Villain

Approximate Time: 45 minutes

Objective: To encourage imaginative and creative thinking, and provide opportunities for self-expression. It is also helpful in learning to develop characters.

Introduction: Encourage each student to consider the name of their super villain, how it will look, act, and what special power it will have. Each super villain should have a vulnerability or weakness in addition to a power. Examples are: Darth Vader who has extraordinary mental powers and super strength, and Ice Man, who turns everything to ice. The super villains we create can not have weapons, blood or other references to violence. And like the superheroes, they must be from your imagination, not those we see on TV or in video games.

Materials: Outline of a human form, paint, glitter, yarn, sequins, buttons, fabric scraps, crepe or tissue paper and anything else that is readily available and would enhance the look of a super villain. If a child draws an animal or ghost-like form, it is also acceptable.

Directions:

- Review the superhero words, the list of superheroes in our community and review qualities of commercial superheroes.
- Pass out non-gendered human form and ask students to create their own villain or bully.
- Each student will present and explain their super villain for the class. The villains will be hung on the wall or bulletin board for the next few weeks. We will call it our Villain's Den or the Bullies Brigade.

Lesson 4

Activity 4.1: Conflict Resolution – Bullies and Villains

Approximate Time: 45 minutes

Objective: Understand the nature of conflict

Materials: Journals, pencils

Introduction: Today we will define conflict. Basically, it is two opposing opinions, behaviors or sets of facts presented simultaneously. Most of us have come to think that conflict is always negative. In fact, there are some very positive aspects to conflict. Believe it or not, conflicts are an opportunity to learn and grow.

Conflicts contain the seeds for turning out positive or negative. It is our individual reaction to these situations that determines either a positive or negative outcome. When we learn the steps to solving a conflict peacefully, it allows us to feel confident in our relationships with others, and gives us a sense of courage, power and respect.

Most disputes between people involve the attempt to meet certain basic social needs we all have for belonging, freedom, fun, and power.

Tell students conflicts often arise because:
- People are trying to meet their own basic needs
- There are limited resources (such as birthday cake, water, money or other supplies).
- People have different values or beliefs.

Divide a piece of drawing paper into thirds and list the following:
- Basic Needs
- Limited Resources
- Values or Beliefs

Ask students to describe a conflict they have witnessed or participated in and assign that conflict to one of the three categories.

Journal Exercise:
Now let's make a list of situations, people and places in our own lives that often lead to conflict.
- Conflicts with friends, parents or siblings
- Conflicts with adults at school or classmates
- Conflicts on the playground, in the cafeteria or hallways at school
- Conflicts in our immediate local area
- Conflicts in the world.

Describe one or two conflicts you have seen or read about regarding superheroes and villains.

Step by step, create an imaginary conflict between your superhero and villain. Write about it in your journal.

Using Batman™ and The Hulk™ as examples, discuss the ways we can be conflicted within ourselves.

Instruct students to write in their journal about an internal conflict they have experienced.

Activity 4.2: Conflict Steps

Approximate Time: 30 minutes

Objective: Understand how conflict occurs.

Introduction: Conflict occurs when two or more people don't agree with each other. There can be very small conflicts and very large ones.

- Do superheroes and villains experience conflict? Why?
- How do they experience it?

Materials: Conflict Steps worksheet on the following page, paper, pencils, pens, crayons.

Directions Part 1:

- Draw both sides of the conflict on a piece of paper that is divided in half.
- Place one person on each side.
- You may use word balloons like you've seen in cartoon books.
- Draw the conflict using the shapes and colors that remind you of conflict and anger.
- One by one, share your drawing with the class.
- Please explain what the conflict is, how the characters in your picture are acting, and tell us whether or not you can think of a more peaceful solution.

Directions Part 2:

- Distribute the conflict steps worksheet. They look like the steps at your school or home. The higher steps represent a high level of conflict and the lower steps represent a low level of conflict.
- Draw one conflict on each step.
- When everyone is done, the conflict steps can be shared.
- What have you learned about conflict and anger today?
- What are some ways to solve a conflict?
- What are some peaceful ways to solve conflicts?
- If you are involved in a conflict that is on a high step, how can you help yourself move down to a lower step?
- If superheroes and villains have conflicts, are there ways they can solve them peacefully

Conflict Steps Worksheet

Top step – high level of conflict

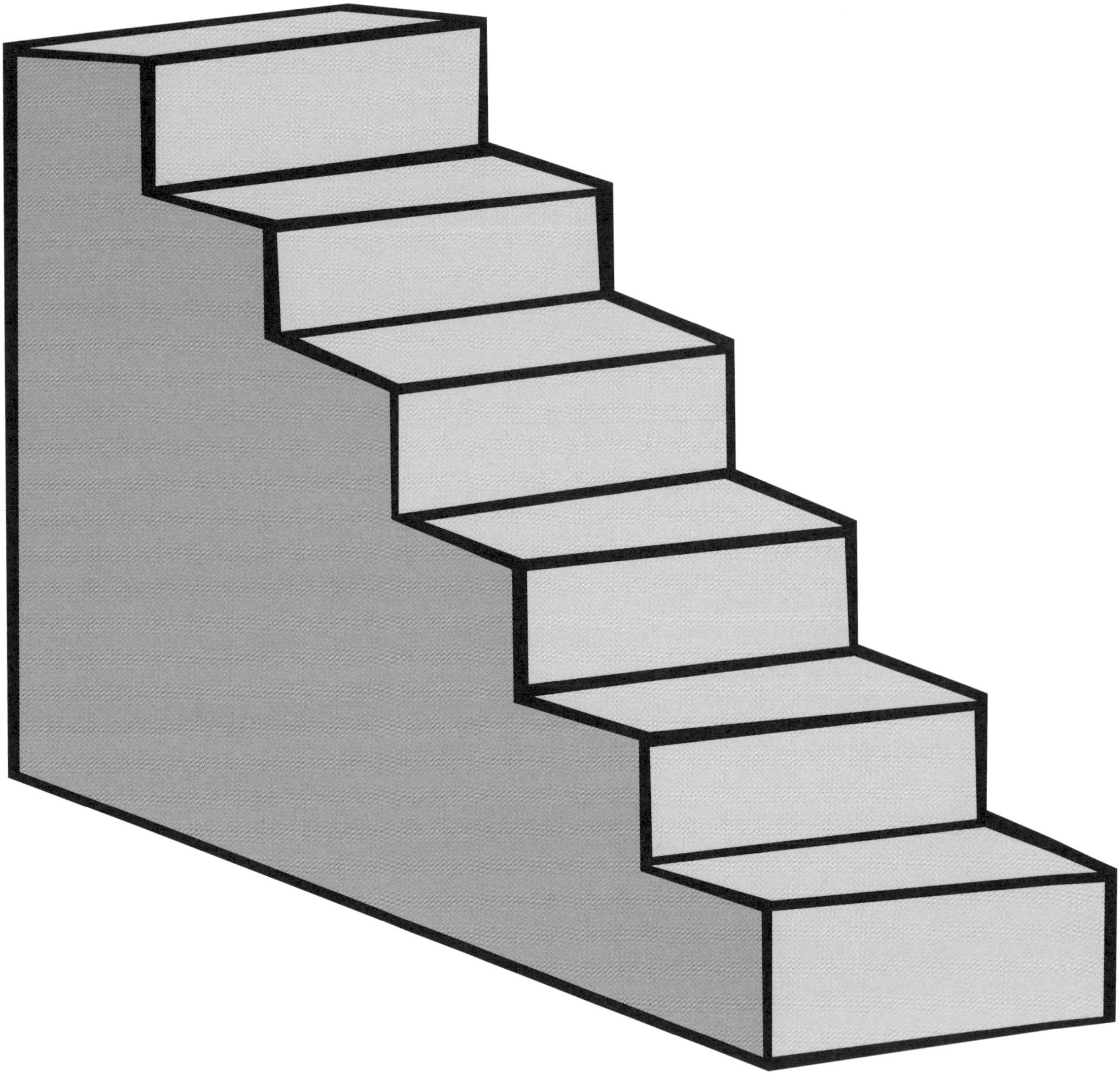

Bottom Step – low level of conflict

Activity 4.3: Superhero Cartoons

Approximate Time: 30 minutes

Objective: To learn how to bring stories and situations to a positive conclusion.

Materials: Create a cartoon worksheet on the following page.

Directions:

- Using the worksheet, draw a cartoon in which the superhero you created has a conflict with the villain you created.
- You will make the cartoon a story using these two characters.
- Share cartoons; help students bring their stories to a positive conclusion using statements from the group lists created in the previous activity.
- How much conflict was involved in each cartoon?
- Did it just arise naturally?

Cartoon Worksheet

Activity 5.1: Superhero/Villain Role Playing Game

Approximate Time: 45 minutes

Objective: Allow students to experience conflict in a safe and playful manner, to reinforce previous lessons, and to learn a new tool for conflict resolution.

Materials: Props, dress up clothes, hats, masks, gloves, etc. Most of these items can be found at a thrift shop, dollar store, or after-Halloween sale.

Directions:
- Show us how superheroes and villains act.
- Break into pairs.
- One of you must be the superhero and the other the villain.
- You must decide what the villain does wrong, how the superhero finds out, what superpower the superhero will use on the villain, how the villain responds, and how the scene will end.
- Use these props and costumes to act it out for the class. This is a play, and no one is allowed to get hurt.
- Therefore, the characters must relate to each other without weapons and powers that really harm.
- You will have 10 minutes to develop your play with your partner. Afterward, we will watch and talk about each play.

Discussion Questions:
- How did these superheroes get their powers?
- How did the villains get their powers?
- How does each of them use their powers?
- Do the superheroes have any weaknesses?
- If so, how do they overcome their weaknesses?

Discussion:
- We've just looked at the conflict between a superhero and a villain. I'm curious; did any of you try to talk through the situation before using your power to destroy the other person? Why or why not?
- If you had the opportunity to talk through a situation before it got too bad, what would you say to someone who was picking on you?

I just gave you a chance to tell me what you might have done.
- Have you ever been in a situation in which you wished you could go back and play it over again?
- Have you ever asked yourself what if I had gone to an adult for help?
- Or what if I had stood up for my friend? (Note for facilitators – have a flip chart available with a list of possible "what if" statements and ask the class to respond to them).

Later on you will have the opportunity to play out the conflict between the villain and the superhero. Next time you're going to have a magic word that can slow the situation down.

This magic word will be your way to summon your powers in a flash. The word is **SUPER.**

Slow Down
Understand the situation
Place yourself in the other's shoes
Encourage other ideas
Respond appropriately

Next time we're going to learn how to use this magic word.

Slow Down

Understand the situation

Place yourself in the other's shoes

Encourage other ideas

Respond appropriately

Activity 6.1: Super Powered Reflector Shields

Approximate Time: 45 minutes.

Objective: Demonstrate how a shield can be used to "slow down" an attack and provide an opportunity to think through a situation, and to gain tools for conflict resolution.

Introduction: Today, we're going to discuss how we can talk to each other during conflict without hurting each other physically or emotionally with words. In addition to your superpowers you're going to have two extra tools at your disposal. We started discussing one, which is the word SUPER so you can call your powers to you. We'll return to that later, but first, you are going to create your own shield to use to repel hurtful words or actions.

- What are shields? Something to protect our bodies in a fight.
- Who uses them? Knights, battleships on Star Trek.
- Shields protect us and can make hurtful things bounce off.
- By protecting us, they give us an opportunity to slow the situation down and respond in an appropriate way.

Materials: heavy cardboard or tag board, aluminum foil, scissors, construction paper, glue. If these materials are not available, the protective shields can be drawn on paper, using any shape each student desires.

Directions:
- Cut cardboard into heart, circle, triangle or rectangular shapes that are two feet wide at the widest section and least 2 feet from top to bottom.
- Have students cover with aluminum foil, smoothing it down as they work.
- Students can then decorate their shield with comforting images, words, color representations or ideas about what they wished they had said in a situation.
- The idea is for the shield to reflect things that make us feel safe and comforted.
- Each student will be asked to show their shield to the class and discuss why they chose their symbols, colors and words.
- If these materials are not available, students can draw their shield on paper and decorate it.

Discussion: Remember the last time we talked about "what if?" Things we might have said or done if only we had the opportunity to slow down and think the situation through before we reacted to it? Those were some of the things you put on your shield. Are there other things you might have said? This shield is a reminder to try and slow down and think before you react in a situation. The other tool we have is the word SUPER. The word SUPER automatically gives you a chance to halt the situation and think it through. As a way to remember what to do when a situation gets bad we're going to assign a word to each of the letters in the command: **SUPER.**

S = Slowdown
- Take a deep breath
- Think before you react

U=Understand the situation
- Am I in real danger?
- What am I feeling?
- What are they feeling?
- Is s/he doing this to look "cool" in front of others?
- Can I find help?

P=Place yourself in their shoes
- Can I handle this by myself?
- What is the other person's goal? Are they trying to hurt me?
- Are they as fearful inside as I am?
- If I were them what would I do?

E=Encourage other ideas.
- Try reasoning the problem out.
- Why do we have to fight about this?
- Is there someone we can go to for help?
- Are there other ways that s/he can look good and I don't get hurt?

R=Respond appropriately
- Make alternative suggestions.
- Make us both win.
- Walk away. Sometimes you can bend but the other person can't.
- Inform an adult.

Directions: Let's look at the situations you acted out with superheroes and villains the other day. We're going to do the same thing today; however, today you can yell the word SUPER to slow the situation down, and raise your shield to deflect physical or vocal attacks. We are going to practice using these tools in the same situation you used the other day.

Today we learned there are alternative ways to resolve an argument or fight if we can slow ourselves down and think. Facilitators who want to read more can refer to The Synaptic Self, by J. LeDoux (2002, p. 213), in which he explains the amygdala hijacking.

Conclusion: Earlier in this program, we discussed ways to slow down a situation and use our shields to deflect. And we played out the situation as if our superheroes were fighting a villain. Tell me, in real life, have any of you been in a situation in which someone was picking on you, or you saw someone else being picked on? What did you do?

Have you ever walked away from that situation and said, "If only I had told an adult about it." Or, "If only I had stood up and said this is not right. If only…"

This is how we can use our shields and the word super in everyday life. The shields don't have to be physically with us, they are part of us all the time. The word SUPER doesn't have to be yelled, although you can if you want to, but you can think it to yourself. Who are other people in our everyday lives who are regular heroes and have to use these tools all the time?

Activity 6.1: The Power of Words

Approximate Time: 30 minutes

Objective: To understand the power of words and their effect on others.

Introduction: The session should open up with a discussion of graffiti – what is it, where do we usually encounter it, why do people do it?

Materials: two large 10 or 12-foot sections of white paper from a roll, markers, paint, crayons.

Directions:

- The class is divided in half. No bad words are allowed.
- One group makes graffiti using the language of villains and evilness, while the other group makes graffiti of superhero terms, positive thoughts and deeds.
- The graffiti session should last about 15 minutes.
- The groups then switch so that everyone has a chance to add to both sets of graffiti.
- The discussion that follows is about the kinds of language each group uses, and the power of words and language in our lives.
- Students should be encouraged to talk about how they felt while using each set of words.
- What feelings did they elicit?

Activity 6.2: Using Anger in Positive Ways – The Super Angerometer

Approximate Time: 30 minutes

Objective: To reinforce "understanding the situation" and not move on before walking a mile in someone else's shoes.

Introduction: Superman™, Batman™, Spiderman™ and many others of our favorite superheroes have become very angry at times. Through their superhero training, they have learned to take the mad feeling of anger and transform it into the positive feeling of helping others, and thus making the world a better place.

- What other superheroes have you seen do this? Harry Potter™, the Hulk™.
- How did they do it? Magic, transforming into their super person.
- Give me an example.
- What was their positive result? They were able to help others.
- How did the superhero feel after turning anger into something positive? Good, energized, cool, empowered.
- What makes you angry?

Think about some situations or people that trigger your anger.

- Where in your body do you feel anger? Perhaps in your forehead or belly?
- What does your face do? Gets hot and red, tightens up.
- What do your hands do? Sweat, clench fists.
- What happens to your voice? It sounds different? Much louder and higher.
- Do your muscles feel tight when you are angry? Yes.
- Do you stand or sit differently? Yes. Sometimes.
- What does the anger make you feel like doing? (See the reproducible anger thermometer on page 35).
- What temperature is your anger today?
- What is the highest temperature you ever had and why?

· What is the lowest anger temperature you have had?
· Are there certain people or activities that make you feel less angry and calmer?
· What caused it to be low? I wasn't angry.
· Can you feel many different temperatures of anger within the same hour?
· The same day?

Materials: Anger Thermometer Worksheet

Take a moment to think about what the anger thermometer of a villain looks like.
· Are their temperatures more or less angry than superheroes? More.
· What makes villains angry? Losing? Not getting what they want? Being punished?
· Are these similar to what makes you or a superhero angry? Yes.
· Where do you think they feel anger in their bodies? Same as me.
· Are they able to turn their anger into something positive? No because they are villains. Give an example.

Anger Thermometer Worksheet

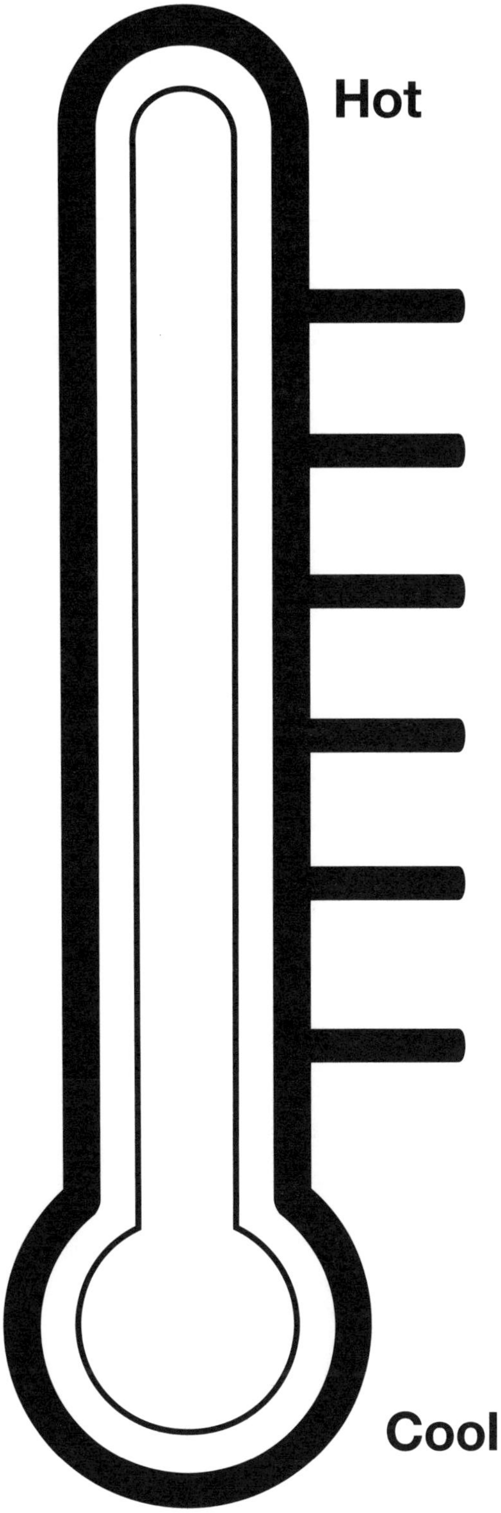

Lesson 7

Activity 7.1: Walk a Mile in My Shoes

Approximate Time: 45 minutes

Objective: To reinforce "P" – Place yourself in someone else's shoes.

Introduction: Who is someone in your real world who you admire? What makes them different from you? What makes them similar? What do you think it would feel like to walk in their shoes?

Materials: The outline of a shoe from the next page, pens, pencils, crayons. Sparkles, glitter, yarn or fabric scraps can also be used.

Directions:

- Each student decorates the outside of the shoe so that it reflects either a superhero or a villain.
- Encourage students to think about what colors, textures and symbols can represent the various points of view.
- Then, each student decorates a shoe to represent the opposite of the first shoe.
- Everyone will have a chance to explain their shoes and their experiences, feelings, and observations about walking in each shoe.
- A variation on this exercise is to divide students into 3 groups. Each group draws a superhero's shoes, a villain's shoe or an innocent bystander's shoe. Students can discuss the characteristics of each character while they work.
- The main object is for students to slow down to understand the shoes they find themselves in and the point of view it represents.

Discussion:

- Did you discover similarities between you and the people whose shoe you tried?
- Describe them.
- How did you feel when you were acting as the other person? Stronger, strange, not sure, etc.
- How did you feel when you returned to being yourself again? Good, comfortable.

As a hero,

- How did it feel to be protecting others and standing up for yourself? Good.
- Do you think you could do this in real life acting as yourself? Maybe.

As the victim,

- Did you feel defenseless? A little, yes, no.
- What did that feel like? Bad, scary.
- Did you feel you had more than one way to engage in the conflict? What are some of the other ways?

As the villain,

- Did you feel powerful? Yes, no, a little.
- Were you ever afraid? Yes, no, a little, a lot.
- Did you ever put yourself in the other person's shoes and think about how your victim felt? Yes, no.
- What are some other ways you might try to get what you wanted?

Now let's go back to when you were a hero and a victim.

- Did you ever think about what it would be like to be the villain? Yes, no, not really.
- After each of these, how did it feel to go back to being yourself? A relief? A disappointment? Hesitant?
- So, in real life can you place yourself in each of these kinds of shoes and help resolve a conflict?

You've placed yourself in the triangle of hero, victim and villain.

- Have you ever been someone who saw a situation but weren't the hero, the victim or the villain? Yes.
- Give me an example.
- What were you feeling? Scared? Threatened?
- What did you do? (Watched, nothing, went to get help)
- Thinking back on it now, what would you do differently? (Stand up for the person, go get help.)
- Notes to facilitators: This is an opportunity to remind people standing on the sidelines, of the impact their role as bystanders has on the situation. If they "egg the bully" on and reward his behavior it makes him stronger. If they stay silent, they are implying permission and silent agreement that they side with the villain or bully.

Shoe Worksheet

Activity 7.2: Emotional First Aid Kit for Superheroes

Approximate Time: 30 minutes

Objective: To reinforce, "E" or "encouraging other ideas."

Materials: Tools template, construction paper, tape, yarn or string, crayons and markers.

Directions: for the First Aid Pouch: Fold construction paper in half and tape the short sides. Decorate your first aid kit and then insert the tools into your kit. If you desire, you can attach a short piece of yarn with tape to use as a handle for your emotional first aid kit.

Make copies of the template for light bulb (bright idea), hand (helping hand), and head (brainstorming), magnifying glass (seeing deeper), bandage (makes it better).

· Think hard about 5 things that help you feel good. It can be people, objects, animals, toys, or even the weather.
· Draw them, cut them out, and place inside your first aid kit. They are there for you whenever you need them.
· Talk about reaching into your own first aid kit when needed.
· Also, first aid and EMS people are superheroes in our own communities.
· How does it feel to give emotional first aid to yourself?
· What is the difference between physical help and emotional help?
· What is it like to give help to someone else? And what is it like when someone else gives you help?

Toolbox Worksheet

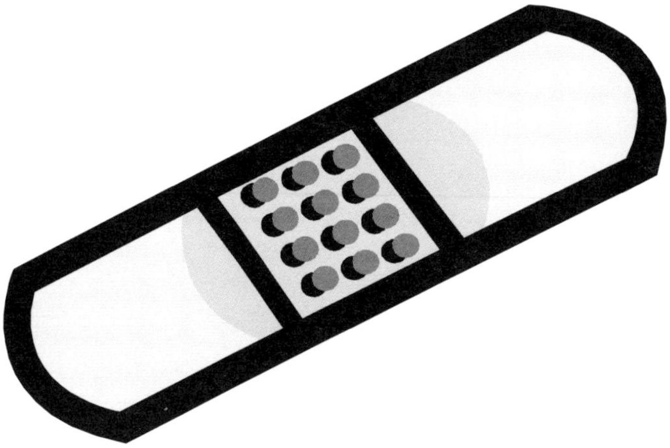

Activity 7.3: The Villain Syndrome

Approximate Time: 30 minutes

Objective: To begin to understand why some people bully others.

Introduction: Let's talk about where you feel your feelings inside yourself. One symptom of the villain disease is a lot of headaches.

· How can you draw that on your villain?
· Stomachaches are another common symptom of this disease. How can you reflect that on your villain?
· How can you show that your villain is feeling unhappy and depressed?
· How can you show the symptom of feeling scared?
· What about the symptom for anger?
· How can you show your villain having trouble sleeping?

Most villains use bullying tactics. Sometimes they act this way mostly because they don't like themselves. Another way to say this is that they have low self-esteem. Not liking yourself can cause aches and pains from holding bad feelings inside, and from feeling angry and afraid most of the time. This time, your human form is going to be a picture of the villain syndrome.

Materials: human form from page 20, crayons, markers, and pencils/pens.

Directions:
· Thinking about everything we've discussed about the Villain Syndrome, draw the symptoms on your human form.
· Use red for anger.
· Use black for being depressed and unhappy.
· Use blue for bullying.
· Use green for feeling afraid and scared

Activity 8.1: The Super Mediator Flexes his Resolution Muscles

Approximate Time: 20 minutes

Objective: To learn how to find the best results for everyone.

Introduction: A mediator is a person who is trained to help people resolve disputes or disagreements. Mediation is a highly developed skill that takes practice, but each of us has the potential to develop this superpower within ourselves. Mediators take a neutral point of view; in other words, they don't take either side of the dispute. They are there strictly for the purpose of helping the opposing forces understand and solve their conflict. It's not an easy job to remain neutral.

Here are some ways to bring conflict to a resolution:

- By slowing down to understand and placing yourself in other's shoes, you can reduce the Emotional heat.
- Compromise is a solution that is in the middle of the opposing sides. It takes elements from both sides and melds them together to form a solution that allows each side to feel they have been heard and responded to. A good example of this is: You take one, and I'll take one.

Here are some additional examples:

- There are two people who want birthday cake but only one piece left. The slice can be cut in half so that each person can have some.
- A brother and sister both want to use the computer, but there is only one. They can each use the computer for 15 minutes.
- Your good friend wants you to come over but you really want him or her to come to your house. Perhaps you could go there today, and s/he can visit you tomorrow.

Negotiating is when both sides look together for a positive alternative that each can live with. Some examples of this are:

- I want to go on vacation to the beach, and the rest of my family wants to go to the mountains. Perhaps we could arrange to go to the beach on the way to the mountains.
- You want to collect your allowance but need to establish what chores you will do in order to earn the allowance. You can throw ideas back and forth until you reach an agreement.

Agreeing to Disagree – Both sides conclude that a resolution is not possible at present, realizing that each viewpoint has validity. The discussion could be tabled for another time when more information is available, more action has been taken, when cooler heads prevail. Some examples of this are:

- I'll push you in the wagon now, and then you can push me.
- We can both agree that we think each of our dads is the best.
- We can't agree, so you play on that side of the playground and I'll play on this side.

By using a mediator at this point in the conflict, you would be encouraging the development of other solutions and ideas that could lead to a peaceful solution.

Activity 8.2: Bully Busters: Cracking the Code of Silence

Approximate Time: 20 minutes

Objective: To understand the role each of us plays in encouraging, and/or stopping bullying behavior by "responding appropriately."

Introduction: Do we agree that no one wants bullying to happen in our classroom or in our school? Does anyone disagree? Can we agree to not tolerate any student hurting another student in a physical or emotional way? Can we further agree that every student has the right to learn in a safe environment? To do that, everyone is expected to follow the rules for good citizenship. If you have rules in your class already, feel free to use them in this activity. We suggest rules such as honesty, being respectful of others; helping to keep yourself and everyone else safe.

As your facilitator, I will take responsibility to investigate whenever one of you lets me know there is bullying going on. You, as students, will be responsible for your own behavior and for reporting behaviors that are not acceptable.

Let's talk about the difference between tattling and reporting. Tattling is when someone tells an adult about something someone did in order to get that person in trouble. Reporting, on the other hand, is when a student lets a responsible adult know there is a problem, either with themselves or with a classmate, for the purpose of protecting that person or themselves. Since kids who bully often make it known that anyone who tells on them will be their next target. There has to be a way you can let an adult know the situation and stay safe. One way is to leave a note without signing your name.

We are going to create a box that will be on the desk in the front of the room. Anyone spotting any kind of bullying or excessive teasing behavior can let me, as your facilitator, know privately, or write a note and stick it in the box. I will go through the box daily to read the notes and act on them. No one besides me will see the notes.

Materials: a shoebox or other cardboard box, sheets of comics from the newspaper, glue, scissors.

Directions:

- I'd like to have a small group of you (perhaps select three students who you want to reward) decorate the box with the comics.
- When you are done, cut a small slit in the top of the box.
- As a group you can brainstorm a name for it.

Activity 8.4: Catch the Bully in the Web

Approximate Time: 20 minutes

Objective: To demonstrate patterns of behavior and to build an awareness of bullying.

Materials: Bully web worksheet on the following page, journals, pencils/pens.

Directions:

- Students should copy the spider web shape onto a blank page in their journals.
- Each student is to write the name of the bully in the center circle.
- Each time the bully says something negative catch it in the web by writing down details of what happened.
- Then find a safe person, either a parent, relative, teacher, counselor, or principal, and discuss your feelings with them.

Spider Web Worksheet

Lesson 9

Activity 9.1: Super Friends: Boosters and Busters

Approximate Time: 30 – 45 minutes

Objective: Understand the rewards and consequences of standing up for friends.

Introduction: Superman™/Clark Kent, Lois Lane and Jimmy Olsen are friends. Batman™/Bruce Wayne and Robin™/Dick Grayson are friends. Spiderman™/Peter Parker and Mary Jane Watson are friends. They stand up for each other and help each other through good times and bad times. Let's explore some characteristics of good and bad friendships.

Think about your best buddies.

- What qualities do they have that you really like?
- What kinds of skills do they have that help you in some way?
- What common interests do you have?
- Do you have any common goals?

Materials: journals, pencils.

Directions:

- Begin writing a list in which each sentence begins with, "A good friend is…."
- See if you can come up with at least 10 sentences about positive friendships.
- Now think about what kinds of things can hurt a good friendship.
- Have any of your friends ever hurt your feelings?
- Have any friends made you feel left out?
- On the other side of the paper, write at least 10 sentences that begin with, "A friend buster does this."
- Are there any similarities between friendship busters and bullies?
- Do you always act one way or the other with your friends, or do you act differently at different times?

Discussion: There are two kinds of bullying. The first is aggressive bullying or direct bullying. Methods of direct bullying include hitting, kicking, throwing things at someone, threatening, teasing and calling names.

The second kind of bullying is indirect or passive bullying. Some methods of this kind of bullying include asking someone else to do the dirty work for you, not including someone on purpose, cyber-bullying or email attacks, whispering secrets to someone when another person is watching and being excluded, and making up or spreading rumors. Can you think of more examples for each type of bullying? Make a class list.

- Before solutions can be found, the emotional heat must be reduced. Use S.U.P.E.R. as a way to slow down and think before you react.

Super Resolution Buster Ideas

- Disagreeing with someone is disrespectful.
- People won't like you if you disagree with them.
- In a conflict, one side always ends up winning, the other side losing.
- Disagreeing with someone is putting them down.
- You can't be friends after a disagreement.

Super Resolution Behaviors Buster

- Disowning, disguising or denying your feelings. Example: "I don't feel angry," or "It was only a joke."
- Don't judge feelings, either yours or someone else's. Example: "You shouldn't feel that way…."
- Don't act out your feelings in a negative or destructive way. Examples include hitting, yelling, punching, throwing things, making threats.

Activity 9.2: Belief Statements about Bullies

Approximate time: 20 minutes

- Let's make a list of possibilities for stopping villains and bullies from hurting others.
- Then let's make a list of belief statements such as, we believe bullying is wrong, or we believe bullies are _______,etc. These lists will be hung near the villains created by students.

Activity 9.3: Bystanders Wear Blinders

Discussion: Bystanders are people who observe something happening. They are the same as witnesses and observers. Bystanders often wear blinders, which are the opposite of the superpower of laser x-ray vision. The reason they can be said to wear blinders is because many times the bystander never reports bullying whether it's being done to themselves or to others. Bullying is an aggressive behavior that causes fear and sometimes harm to others. Bullies tend to repeat their behavior over time. The main cause of bullying is low self-esteem. This means the bully doesn't feel good about her/himself or like her/himself very much.

- Who remembers what the acronym "S.U.P.E.R." stands for?
- If you see someone on the playground being bullied what could/should you do?
- Do you run to an adult for help?
- Do you run away from the bully?
- Do you try to help the victim?
- Do you feel you should ignore it because it's none of your business?

Activity 9.4: No Bullying Allowed Buttons

Approximate Time: 30 minutes

Objective: Reinforce "R"- responding appropriately and make a positive statement against bullying behavior.

Materials: plastic button sets from an art supply catalog or craft supply store. They usually come with the paper for decorating inside and have a pin back so students can wear them. If you can't get them from a catalog, you can cut out circles about 3 inches wide and have them laminated when they are complete. Tape can be used to stick them on students, either double sided tape, Velcro or regular tape made into a circle.

Directions: To change the bullying climate in your school, the entire school has to be involved so that everyone gets the message that there is zero tolerance for bullying. One way to get your message to the entire school is to wear special buttons you make yourself.

- Think for a few minutes about exactly what message you think will help others understand that bullying will not be tolerated in this school.
- How can you represent it in words and pictures?
- Draw your message.
- When you are done, you can ask for help pinning it onto your shirt.

Lesson 10

Activity 10.1: Super TV News Reporters

Approximate Time: 30 – 45 minutes

Objective: Learning to describe conflict in a non-emotional way.

Introduction: Each student takes notes on this discussion in their journal, writes a short news report on one conflict, and then goes inside the TV to report the story.

Materials: a large cardboard box with a TV screen cut out of one side. The box can be decorated with wallpaper scraps, colored paper, or paint. A globe is helpful to have on hand.

Directions: Have students take turns as the super TV news reporter and talk about the following:

· Are there events in our community that involve major conflicts?

· Tell about conflicts in other parts of the world.

· How are they being solved? War, aggression, yelling, talking.

· For example, do they all involve battles?

· Take note of where in the world these conflicts are taking place. If you have a globe or a world map, point them out to students.

Follow up:
· What is it like to report on conflicts which are happening around our country and other parts of the world?

· Do you agree with the way these conflicts are being solved?

Activity 10.2: Superheroes Take Responsibility for Their Feelings

Approximate Time: 20-30 minutes

Objective: To learn the difference between aggressive and assertive behavior.

Discussion: When a conflict arises, some people react by being forceful and pushy. That is called being aggressive. Villains often act aggressively. Other people react by retreating or doing nothing. That is known as being passive.

You can be a superhero by standing up for yourself if someone bullies you. That is called being assertive. One way of being assertive is using "I" statements. (Write examples on board). Sometimes it doesn't feel natural to make "I" statements, but with practice, it will become automatic. "You" statements, such as, "You never want to play with me any more", sound accusing. They increase the amount of conflict, because they make the recipient of the statement defensive. When someone feels defensive, they feel attacked, blamed, and feel they need to defend themselves.

As you are leading this discussion, draw a line on the board with passive at one end and aggressive on the other end. Assertive will be in the middle, demonstrating that assertive is a balance between the two.

Material: Journals, pencils/pens.

Directions: We are going to write 10 "I" sentences. Examples of an "I" sentence could be, "I don't like it when you leave me out of a game," or, "I feel angry when you cut in front of me when we're in line." After we practice writing "I" sentences, we will act them out in pairs of two.

On the back of the paper, write 5 "you" statements. Share them with the class. Ask students which statements are best to use when needing to confront others.

Introduce a behavior of a bully you want to stop. Say it in a "you" statement first, then in an "I" statement. Which do you think is more likely to inspire a bully to change?

Activity 10.3: Super Body Language

Approximate Time: 20 – 30 minutes

Objective: To understand how we communicate beyond words and language.

Materials: none.

Introduction: We are going to discuss the way our bodies tell others a lot about how we are feeling. This is known as body language. Have you ever noticed that some people speak louder than others? Some people stand up very straight, and others slouch. Some people can't look you in the eye; others speak so softly you can hardly hear them. People whose body language tells others they are confident and care about themselves, are less likely to be bullied by other kids.

Directions: Now we are going to look at the superheroes we have created and make a list of the body language they use to let people know they are self-confident. We will hang the list near our superheroes.

Lesson 11

Activity 11.1: Peaceful Alternatives

Approximate Time: 20 minutes

Objective: Reinforce "R" – Responding Appropriately

Introduction: Let's examine some of the concepts we've looked at up until this point. This is a discussion about violence vs. peaceful solutions to conflict. Some of the questions we will address in this important discussion are:

- What exactly is a conflict? (Use definition from Lesson 4).
- Do superheroes always solve their conflicts with violence? No.
- What are some examples of violent solutions in the world?
- How does a peaceful solution affect each person in the conflict?
- What are some violent ways to solve a conflict? Make a list.
- Do these methods work?
- Why or why not?
- What are some peaceful ways superheroes solve conflicts?
- What are the benefits of solving a disagreement in a peaceful way?
- What are some peaceful ways you solve a conflict? Make a class list.
- How do these methods affect the victim? The bully? The superhero?
- Does anyone win?
- What does it mean to win?
- Can we agree that cooperating will lead to less bullying?
- What does it mean to cooperate? (Everyone wins).
- How does it make people feel to create a solution to a conflict that benefits everyone?
- How can you help others succeed if they are having trouble?
- What are random acts of kindness? Make a list.
- Can we conclude that one method works better than the other? Why?
- Can you be a peaceful superhero in your life and with your friends?
- How can you do that? Each child records their list in their journal.

Activity 11.2: Superheroes & Villains Working it Out

Approximate Time: 45 minutes.

Objective: Learning the value of negotiating a win/win situation

Materials: paper folded so there are 6 boxes of equal size, pencils. Each student will fill 3 sheets of paper.

Directions:
- Using the comic strip paper, draw a story about a conflict between a superhero and a villain.
- The first cartoon should illustrate aggression, the second should show passivity, and the third cartoon should show assertiveness.

Discussion Questions:
- Discuss the differences between the three styles of handling a conflict.
- Which one do you do most often?
- Which style do you use least often?
- Which one would you like to improve upon?

Activity 11.3: The World of the Peaceful Place

Approximate Time: 45 minutes

Objective: To develop a safe place available to everyone.

Materials: journals, crayons/colored pencils.

Discussion: As a group, we are going to decorate a corner of the room and call it our Peaceful Place. Using crayons, paint, or markers, draw a superhero in a peaceful place. Use the colors you feel are peaceful. When you are done, each of you will be able to share your special place with the rest of the class. We will use these pictures to decorate the Peaceful Place.

This will be a place to go if you are feeling sad or angry. As you sit there, you can honor your feelings by realizing that these are natural emotions, and everyone feels them at different times. There are superhero buttons in the Peaceful Place, which can be used to help you to feel good again. Hopefully after sitting in the Peaceful Place for a few minutes you will feel better and be able to return to your class.

- What does peace mean?
- What does peace feel like?
- Where do you feel it in your body?
- What colors remind you of peace?
- What kind of music makes you feel peaceful?
- Can you think of some peaceful situations?
- What is the opposite of peace?
- How do superheroes help keep the peace?

Directions: Have students think about what their special peaceful place looks like and have them draw it in their journals.

Lesson 12

Superheroes Working in Teams

Introduction: This begins the teambuilding section of this program. Earlier in this program, we tried on shoes to see how it felt to be a hero, a victim, and a villain. We also briefly discussed being the person on the sidelines. In reality, each of those roles is a participant, even if they are silent. Now we will talk about how much stronger we can be when we all work together.
Some questions to start your classroom discussion are:

- Can you name some superheroes that worked in teams? (Batman and Robin, the Justice League.)
- What does it mean to be a member of a team? (Working together, using the strengths of each member to work toward a common goal.)
- Who makes the rules? (The leader, everyone)
- What if there is no leader? (The group decides, chaos can take over)
- What if one person disagrees with the rest of the team? (We have to work it out; they pout and demand)
- What happens when the goals of team members become more important than the goals of the team? (Everything falls apart; we get different results from what was originally intended.)

Activity 12.1: Connectedness: We Are All in this Together

Approximate Time: 20 minutes

Objective: Learning Cooperation

Materials: a ball of string

Directions:
- Have the group stand in a circle.
- Select one person as the starting connector. Have students share one thing that describes working together.
- The starter holds the end of the string in one hand, and tosses the ball to someone else.
- Person #2 then repeats the same thing by holding the string with one hand and tossing the ball to someone else, anywhere in the circle, while sharing something different to describe working together.
- When everyone has caught the ball of string, look at the design to see how you are all connected.

Discussion:
- What does it mean to be connected? Tied together.
- Does it mean we are all dependent upon one another? No.
- How did you feel when the ball came to you? Nervous.
- How did you feel as you threw the ball to someone else? Nervous that I'd mess up. Relieved my turn was over.
- Facilitator's Note: Repeat the ball toss, having each person throw it to some different than before. When everyone has caught the ball, look at the new pattern as a group. Are there any similarities to the previous pattern? Do you see any differences?

Activity 12.2: Dynamo Team Drawings

Approximate Time: 30 minutes

Objective: Introduce teambuilding concepts.

Materials: paper, pencils.

Directions:

- Assign each student a partner for this exercise.
- Students are asked to communicate with each other strictly through pictures, using no vocalizations, words, letters or numbers.
- The room should be very quiet. Each pair is given a charades-type clue.
- Afterward, the roles are reversed and the opposite person is the artist and the other will guess.

Discussion:

- Students are encouraged to talk about how they felt during this exercise. The team approach is discussed.
- How did it feel to communicate non-verbally?
- Was it difficult to read your partner's body language?
- Did you and your partner work well together?
- Could your team approach be improved? How?

Here are some suggestions for charades to be given out on slips of paper include:

Costume	Team	Castle
Spaceship	Villain	Hero
Magic wand	Cape	Mask
Rainbow	Scared	Excitement
Conflict	Top secret	X-ray vision
Leadership	Superpower	Bully

Lesson 13

Activity 13.1: Super Mission Quest

Approximate Time: 90 minutes

Objective: Practice team building and working together for a common goal.

This exercise is a key piece of this program. We suggest you set aside either an entire afternoon or at least several periods in order to get the maximum effect. If you aren't able to schedule the activity in this way, we suggest you use the haunted house as a stopping point for the day since the superheroes will be staying there.

In order for this exercise to be optimal, each team should have an adult working with them to record the strategy and its outcome, as well as to observe behaviors of each team member to be used in the concluding discussion.

Introduction:
Have any of you heard of the Justice League™? Describe for me what the Justice League™ does. (They work together to fight bad guys.) What we're going to do today is similar. We're going to divide your superhero characters into teams. Each team is on a quest to save humanity. You can do this by taking advantage of the power of your teammates. You can only use the power of your superhero once to solve the mission on the quest.

Materials: Map from page 54, large newsprint paper, markers.

Directions:
· Count off by 6 and gather into groups (this way the classes are thoroughly mixed).
· The facilitator reads the following to students:

There is potential disaster in the air. The largest cruise ship in the world has landed near the island. In the ship are two dozen of the world's most brilliant scientists. They know a secret: the largest asteroid in the universe is on a collision course for Earth. It is larger than the Earth.

These scientists believe that when it hits Earth, our planet will crumble into billions of pieces. They believe no one will survive. It is due to hit Earth late tomorrow afternoon.

The scientists also believe there is a secret passageway somewhere on this island leading to a time warp. If they can find the time warp before the asteroid hits, there is a chance that the Earth and all its inhabitants can survive.

Only you and your team can save the day and you must do it as a group. If any team members are left behind you will not succeed in saving the Earth. But how can you possibly do that? You will have to work as a team to figure out a way. This is good opportunity to use your active listening skills to clarify each other's ideas.

Think for a minute about what your individual strengths are. What things do you do well? Perhaps you are a good thinker, a good problem solver or a good friend. These are all strengths that you bring to your team. Each of you as a superhero has a superpower. In order to save the Earth, each team member must use their strength, and each of you can only use your superpower once.

Each team will be given a map, containing information about safe and lethal sections of the island. Your team needs to get to the island, climb a steep cliff and face other obstacles in order to survive.

The only thing anyone knows for sure is that the final impediment to reaching the time warp is a plate that requires the handprint of each member of the team at the exact same time.

Students are given about 20 minutes to figure out their strategy, and then one person from each group will report the team strategy. Each group member will tell the class what strengths they added to their team and how that helped the team effort.

Expanded version – each team chooses one item at a time from a table of 20 props, keeping in mind that:
(a) they would have to rely on these tools in order to survive on the island for a week,
(b) they were required to survive as a team,
(c) they must utilize everyone's strengths to survive.

Props included a blanket, a hat, hand shovel, rope, pulley, scissor, soap, string, toilet paper, an empty box carton, etc. When all items are distributed, each team should have 5 props to work with. In conclusion, team members will include how they used their props in order to survive.

Discussion:

- How did you feel when you thought the Earth was going to be destroyed? Scared.
- So, what happened? We used everyone's strengths, worked together, zapped someone, etc.
- Could you have done it alone? No.
- What challenges did you face?
- How did you use each other's strengths?
- How did you make decisions about what to do next? We voted, he told us what to do, we drew straws, etc.
- Did one person take control? Yes, no.
- Did you all pitch in equally? Yes, no, sometimes.
- Did you treat each other as true equals? Yes, no, sometimes.

Map Worksheet

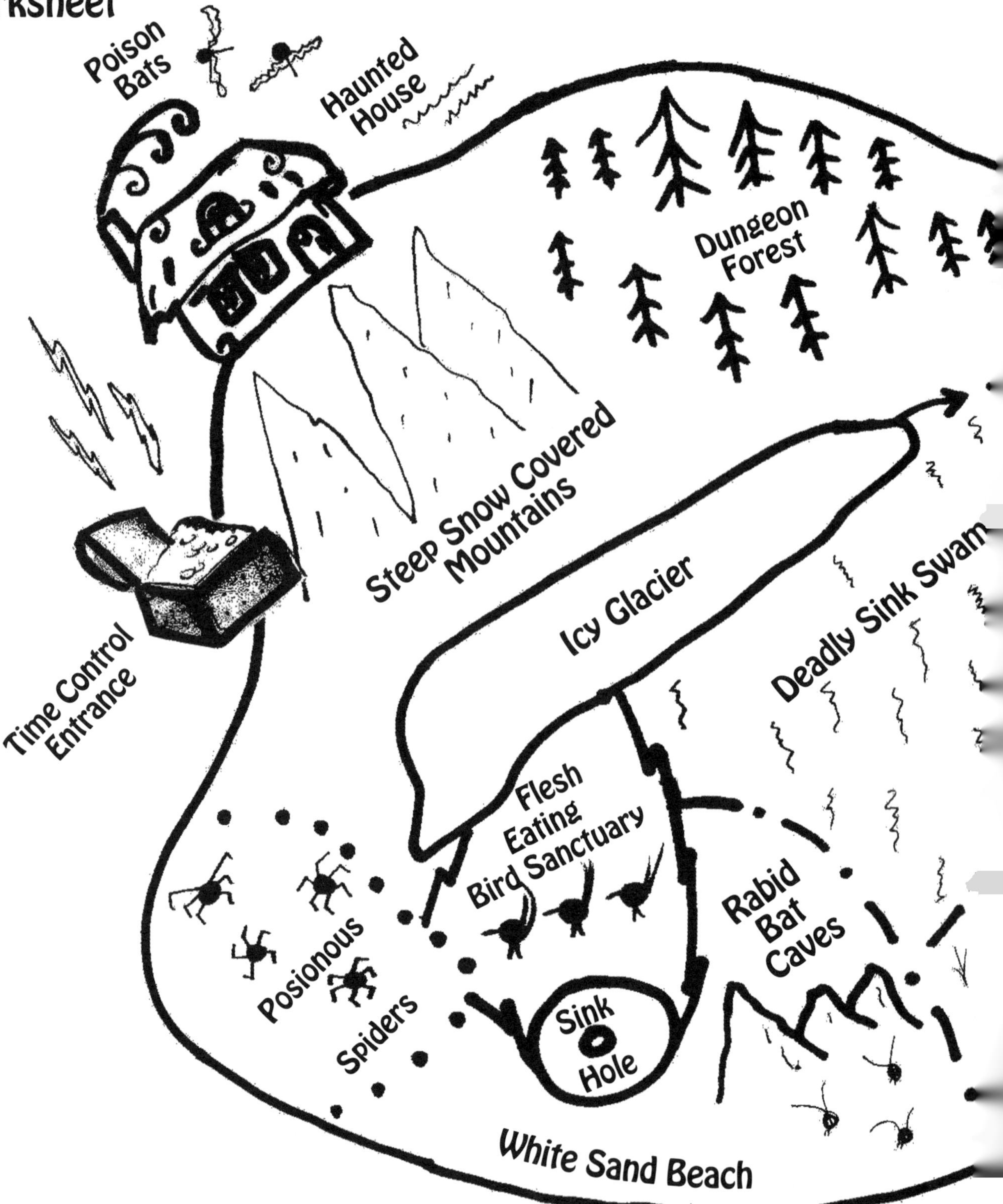

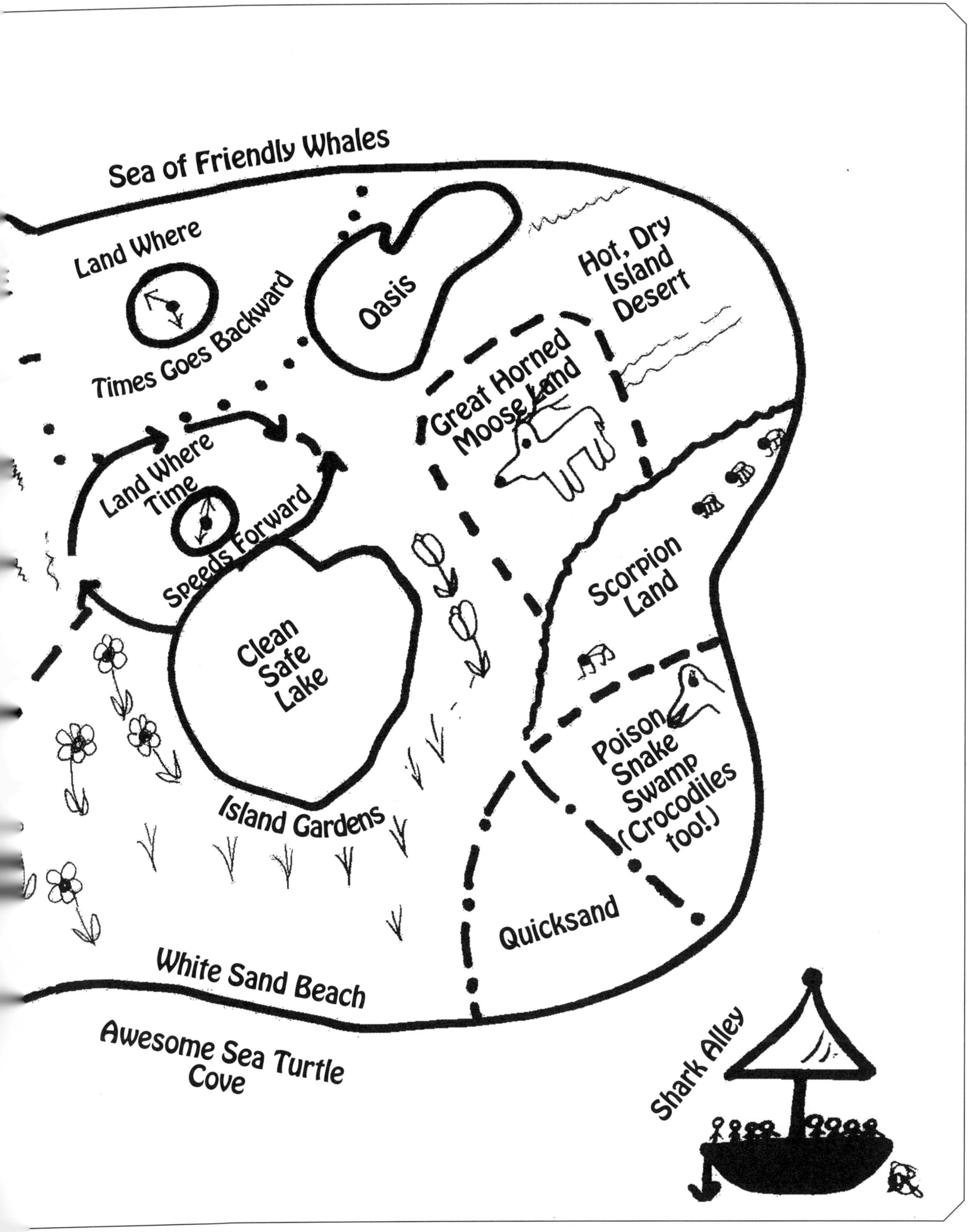
Sea of Friendly Whales
Land Where
Times Goes Backward
Oasis
Hot, Dry Island Desert
Great Horned Moose Land
Land Where Time
Speeds Forward
Clean Safe Lake
Scorpion Land
Poison Snake Swamp (Crocodiles too!)
Island Gardens
Quicksand
White Sand Beach
Awesome Sea Turtle Cove
Shark Alley

Activity 13.2: Planet Explosion

Approximate Time: 30 Minutes

Objective: To reinforce cooperating as a group.

Materials: a large space with moveable furniture.

Directions:

- Assign various injuries to half the students, which they will act out.
- The other half will be the superheroes.
- The planet we are on has just exploded. Many of our group members have injuries. We don't have time to figure out what happened; we must get everyone to safety quickly.
- There is a cave not far from here (the other side of the room). Before the exercise begins, place obstacles (desks, chairs overturned, etc.) between the cave and the site where the injured lie.
- The superheroes must move everyone to the cave safely and without further injury. They can do this by holding the person's hand and walking with them. No one should physically pick up another person.

Discussion:

- How did you feel when you realized there was an explosion?
- How did the superheroes feel about helping others get to safety?
- What were the challenges?
- How did the injured feel being helped by the superheroes?
- Did the superheroes work together as a team?
- Why or why not?
- What did it feel like to be in a cave knowing the planet exploded?

Lesson 14

Activity 14.1: Team Building Blocks

Approximate Time: 30 minutes.

Objective: To continue to reinforce team concepts.

Introduction: Students build a superhero fort to learn teambuilding skills. The rules for this team building exercise are:
- Everyone has a turn
- Everyone is respectful to everyone else and to their ideas and contributions
- Everyone gives a compliment when someone finishes a turn.

Materials: sets of building blocks, large newsprint paper, tape

Directions: The class is divided into groups of 4. One member of the group is chosen to be the observer. The facilitator tells students that each team must build a superhero fort to have their meetings in with the blocks, and they must do it within two minutes. No superpowers can be used to build the fort.

As each team works, their observer is watching the way team members are reacting to each other, whether:
- The group was cooperative or uncooperative with one another
- Each person participated equally
- One person was dominant, etc.

As a next step, a set of rules written on newsprint paper are taped to the wall and reviewed.

The groups are then asked to build something new in two minutes while following the rules. The observer summarizes the group's behavior according to the criteria above. Have teams display their forts and talk about how they decided to make it.

Discussion:
- What difference do rules make? They provide guidelines and help keep order.
- Are rules good or bad? They can be both.
- What if a team member doesn't want to participate? You can find ways to encourage everyone to participate.
- Conversely, what if one team member is very dominant? Sometimes that is OK. Encourage them to open the discussion for everyone to participate.

Activity 14.2: A Super Zapper

Approximate Time: 20-30 minutes.

Objective: To gain understanding that success is easier when people work together.

Materials: several small or medium sized balls.

Directions:

- Divide students into teams of 6.
- Each team is given a foam ball and asked to toss the ball from person to person.
- The chemical composition of the ball can zap superpowers so you won't want to hold it for long.
- If the ball drops, it takes everyone's superpowers away and you're forced to do a complete round to earn back your superpowers.
- The leaders then increase the stress level by urging them to pass faster and faster without dropping the ball.
- For the final round, if a team drops the ball they are out.

(Leaders should observe, and later comment on, how the teams worked together. Did they move closer to each other? Did they offer encouragement? Did they develop a pattern? Did the stress cause more mistakes to happen? Etc.)

Discussion:

- How did it feel at the beginning of this exercise? (Confusing, ok.)
- How did you feel as the pressure increased? (Nervous.)
- How do you think your team members felt? (The same.)
- How did your team feel when you dropped the ball and were disqualified? (They all blamed me, Maggie said it was alright.)
- Was anyone blamed? (Yes.)
- How did that feel? (Bad.)
- Were there things the team could have worked on to improve? (Yes.)
- Like what? (Working together, encouraging each other.)
- Was everyone doing his or her absolute best? (Yes.)

Lesson 15

Activity 15.1: Superhero Helping Hands Mural

Approximate Time: 30 minutes.

Objective: To understand that everyone can be a hero; especially when they work together in a community.

Materials: colored paper, large sheet from a roll of white paper, paint, markers, crayons.

Directions:
- Have each student trace his/her hand on a piece of colored paper.
- Students should decorate the hand to reflect themselves.
- Write on each finger a way they help people.
- The hands will be pasted to the mural paper, and hung in the classroom or hallway
- Students should be encouraged to share the ways in which they are a helping hand.

Discussion: Today's program is a transition to an understanding that everyone can be a hero; especially when they work together in a community. We discussed Clark Kent, Bruce Wayne and Peter Parker as doing good things for others without having special powers. They are just regular people like us. Let's make a list of the superheroes in our own community, and in our country. (Fireman, policemen, ambulance drivers, parents, teachers, senators, government, etc.)

- What makes them heroes? They like to do good for others.
- Have you ever been a hero? Yes, no.
- What made you a hero? I stood up for my friends; I helped my parents with my baby brother.
- How were you different than you are right now? I wasn't.

Activity 15.2: Superhero Buttons

Approximate Time: 30 minutes

Objective: To discover everyone has the power to be a hero.

Materials: plastic button kits, markers, colored pencils. Plastic button sets from an art supply catalog or craft supply store. They usually come with the paper for decorating inside and have a pin back so students can wear them. If you can't get them from a catalog, you can cut out circles about 3 inches wide and have them laminated when they are complete. Tape can be used to stick them on students, either double sided tape or regular tape made into a circle.

Directions:
- Students are asked to decorate their button with themselves as a superhero.

Program Conclusion:
This is the end of the program for this school year.
- What did you learn?
- What were your favorite parts?
- What were your least favorite parts?
- Does anyone have any other ideas about working with superheroes?
- Other activities you would like to do?
- Think about the superhero you are and what strengths you added to your team. Draw yourself as a superhero on your button with the words: I'm a superhero!

Certificate of Completion

This certificate is being presented to

____

For 15 weeks of participation in *Superheroes Unmasked*

____
DATE

____
NAME OF SCHOOL, GRADE

Superheroes Unmasked

Superhero, Bystander, Villain Role-Play

Approximate Time: 45 minutes.

Objective: To understand that there are often more than two sides to a conflict.

Directions:

- Break up into partnerships of three and plan a skit in which one person is the villain or bully, one is the superhero and the third person is the bystander. They are having a conflict, and are asked to act it out.
- The bystander has to decide how to react to the other two. This should take 10 - 15 minutes.
- Each group performs their skit for the class.

Discussion:

- Who is the victim?
- How does it feel to be the victim?
- Have you ever felt that way before?
- How could you tell who was the superhero, who was the villain and who was the middle character?
- Did the middle character automatically function as a mediator?
- Ask each character in the skit how they felt deep down inside as the conflict was going on — what range of emotions did they feel?
- What physical sensations did it cause (stomachache, headache, etc.) Discuss the difference and the interplay between physical and emotional symptoms.

Look out: The Cowboys and Indians are Here

Approximate Time: 45 minutes.

Objective: To practice mediation skills.

Introduction: Cowboys and Indians are a very important part of our history. Conflicts between the cowboys and Indians are in cartoons, on TV, movies, books and computer games.

· What kind of conflicts did they have?
· What did they fight about?
· How did they act during a conflict?
· Do you think one side was bad and the other side was good?
· Were there some good points about each side?
· If so, what were they?
· If you could have been on one side, which one would you pick?
· Why?
· What would be alternative ways for cowboys and Indians to handle their conflicts?

Materials: Cowboy and Indian cutouts, crayons.

Directions: Everyone is to cut their cowboy and Indian out, color them, and have them on their desks.Your superhero is going to help solve the conflict.

Discussion Questions:
· How could this happen?
· What kind of words does s/he use?
· What kind of actions does s/he use?
· Is the superhero fair to both sides?
· How does the situation end?
· Can it be worked out so that everyone wins?

Hand Tracings

Approximate Time: 20 minutes

Objective: To understand the individual personality and how it fits within a Group.

Materials: construction paper, markers or crayons and banner paper.

Directions:
· Each person traces and decorates their hand in a way they feel represents themselves.
· Students cut out his/her hand and paste it onto the banner paper, which has the headline: Superheroes of "class name" or grade.
· A discussion follows on the nature of the designs chosen to represent each person and the choices for placement on the paper within the group at large.
· Group dynamics are explored.

Discussion:
· Tell me why you decorated your hand the way you did. Why did you choose the colors and designs you did?
· Tell me why you placed your hand in the spot you picked.
· What are the similarities between the hands on the banner?
· What are the differences between the hands?
· Looking at the entire banner, what is the relationship between the hands?

Whiz Kid's Laser Vision Glasses

Approximate Time: 20 minutes

Objective: To understand that emotions change during conflict.

Materials: Tag board or file folders, tissue paper in various colors, scissors, glue, glasses template on next page.

Directions:

- Using the laser vision glasses template have students color and cut the glasses out.
- Precut different colors of tissue paper according to the template, so the tissue paper fits into the glasses.
- Have students think about what color different emotions remind them of. For example: What color is happiness to you? What about Sadness? Worrying? Silly? Embarrassed? Shy? Afraid? Angry?
- Have students lightly tape the colored tissue paper into the glasses so that it can be changed over and over again.Using the emotions listed above, talk about how it feels to see the world through various colors of emotion.
- Which color laser glasses do you think superheroes wear?
- What color glasses do you think villains wear?
- If someone is laughing at you what color would you wear? Why?
- If you were to be involved in a conflict what color would you wear? Why?
- If you were a bystander what color would you wear? Why?

Laser Vision Worksheet

Recipe for Kryptonite

Approximate Time: 15 minutes to assemble, takes three days to fully grow.

Objective: To tie a science project into superhero play.

Materials: 1 sponge or cotton balls, 4 Tbs. liquid bluing, 4 Tbs. water, 1/3 cup salt, green food coloring, small glass bowl.

Directions:
- If using a sponge, cut into several pieces and place in bowl.
- Mix 2 Tbs. Salt with bluing and water.
- Pour over sponge or cotton. Leave to grow for 1 day.
- On day 2, sprinkle 2 more Tbs. of salt over the forming crystals.
- On day 3, add 2 more Tbs. salt, and a few drops of food coloring on each sponge or cotton ball.
- You can even play around with the food coloring to create a mottled effect.

Superhero Slime

Approximate Time: 30 minutes

Objective: To tie a crafts project into superhero play.

Materials: talcum powder, glue, distilled water, food coloring, borax, paper cups.

Directions:
- Place 1 teaspoon of powder in each cup.
- Add 5 teaspoons of glue, 4 teaspoons of distilled water, and a few drops of food coloring to the cup.
- Mix a solution of borax using 1 tablespoon for each cup of distilled water.
- Add 1 teaspoon to each cup, stir.
- When mixture is thoroughly mixed, remove the crime scene slime from the cup. The slime becomes less sticky the more it is handled. It can be stored in sealable bags or airtight containers until the next crime scene investigation. It can be used to collect fingerprints, DNA samples, and other crime solving clues, or to just play with.

The Hero in You

Approximate Time: 30 minutes

Objective: Using music as a way to connect students to their emotions.

Materials: a copy of the song *Hero* by Mariah Carey (Copyright by Sony Music), cassette or CD player, and Superman™ *(It's Not Easy)* by John Ondrasik, Five For Fighting (Copyright by Sony Music), drawing paper and crayons or colored pencils.

Directions:
- Ask students to close their eyes or put their heads down on their desk and relax while they listen to this song, paying careful attention to the words.
- After the song is over, encourage students to think about the messages in the song, and then draw what it made you think about and how the song made you feel.
- Each child then presents their drawing to the class and gives a short explanation.

My Superpowers: X-Ray Vision

Approximate Time: 30 minutes

Objective: To discover that we all are similar and yet unique at the same time.

Materials: paper outlines of a human form, crayons, markers, other decorative items.

Introduction: Congratulations! You have been granted the superpower of X-ray vision for today. It will be fun to discover ways to use this new power. But, remember, along with power comes responsibility.

Directions:
- On the front of the human outline, draw yourself as a hero.
- Take a few minutes to think about how your teachers, classmates, friends and family see you when you do something good for others.
- Decorate the form to reflect the way you think others think about you.
- Using the superpower of X-ray vision you have been given for today, on the opposite side of the paper, draw the way you see yourself on a normal day.
- Take a few minutes to think about things you like and dislike about yourself.
- Then think of ways to decorate the form to look the way you see yourself.
- When everyone is done, we will share both sides of you one by one.
- Are there other people who look similar on the outside as you do?
- Are there others who look similar to you on the inside?
- Discuss the similarities and differences that make each of us unique human beings.

Super Spidery Brainstorm - Problem Solving

Approximate Time: 30 minutes

Objective: To understand that there are many sides to a problem and different solutions available.

Materials: paper and pencil/pen, or blackboard

Directions:
- This exercise is about brainstorming and how the process of brainstorming can solve problems, help us look at things differently, and come up with new ideas.
- Brainstorming is following your thoughts so that you can come up with words or ideas that are similar but slightly different. Goals drive behavior.
- You can make a diagram out of a brainstorm, and it might look like a spider web.
- For example, you put the main word in the center of the web, and for each line of the web, write in the next word that comes to mind.
- Let's start with the center which says, My Superpowers.
- Each person will work on their own web to brainstorm ideas about their own special talents and abilities.
- Usually one thought leads to another, so follow those thoughts as you work your way to the outer part of the web. After everyone is done, we will put a master list on the board and talk about heroes.
    - What is the problem?
    - What have you already tried in order to solve it?
    - How do you want me to help?

Journal Exercise: Advertising Your Superpowers

Time: 30-45 minutes

Objective: To discover personal strengths and discuss them in a positive manner.

Materials: Journals or lined paper, pencils.

Directions:

- Students are encouraged to concentrate on their major strengths and positive traits, Pretend you are creating an advertisement for yourself and that you want to sell yourself to the world.
- You can use a headline, a slogan, logo, or nickname.
- Students having difficulty can be helped individually.
- Try to help students make as complete a list as possible, as this list will be the basis of other exercises.
- Spend as much time on this exercise as it takes to make a reasonably sized list and write or draw them.
- Ads are shared with the class and a discussion follows about the unique qualities of each of us.

Hero's Word Find #1

P	O	P	C	G	P	L	A	Y	X
B	L	A	O	I	E	M	F	I	A
Y	G	L	O	B	A	L	P	K	M
U	L	M	V	N	C	J	M	E	N
W	I	C	A	P	E	S	T	S	N
S	A	W	J	R	V	P	R	E	T
P	O	D	Y	O	Z	Z	M	A	P
Q	B	A	N	T	B	P	A	O	I
T	L	A	S	E	R	G	S	O	X
H	E	A	D	C	E	F	T	B	R
M	J	U	S	T	I	C	E	Y	A
N	O	G	A	Y	C	D	R	A	Y
O	K	N	D	M	E	G	M	G	D
P	E	B	E	A	R	W	I	N	P
R	R	I	G	H	T	F	N	D	K
S	V	C	O	M	N	P	D	O	V

Pop	Go	Mastermind
Laser	Joker	Justice
Right	Ray	Ice
Do	Sad	Map
Win	Play	Oz
Pal	Pod	Ok
Peace	Capes	Yikes
Protect	Men	Global

Mastermind Word Find #2

C	A	P	T	A	I	N	X	S	W
R	R	F	R	F	G	I	B	C	M
I	S	T	U	A	E	C	Y	A	P
M	X	O	T	P	M	E	T	R	O
E	U	V	H	I	Y	L	E	E	W
F	L	Y	D	L	N	E	R	D	S
I	R	E	S	E	B	Y	A	B	U
G	H	A	Y	S	W	Y	D	U	R
H	E	R	O	E	S	D	I	C	V
T	F	L	Q	B	I	C	O	B	I
E	M	N	W	E	S	U	T	E	V
R	E	V	E	N	G	E	I	Q	A
S	E	I	B	U	O	S	T	D	L
A	W	D	S	T	L	G	S	I	Y
C	R	U	S	A	D	E	R	O	W
Z	U	H	J	K	L	P	R	X	W

Captain
Gold
Crime fighters
Fly
Metro
revenge

Nice
Revenge
Heroes
Nerds
Truth

Crusader
Survival
Radio
Year
Scared

Crime Fighters Word Find #3

P	A	S	S	W	O	R	D	S	U
L	B	E	F	I	H	N	A	H	A
A	Y	C	M	N	E	K	E	I	T
N	E	R	D	U	S	U	P	E	R
E	M	E	K	Z	H	X	K	L	S
T	O	T	R	U	S	T	U	D	D
S	O	S	F	Q	M	R	E	L	F
A	E	I	K	W	R	O	N	G	E
F	Q	A	D	E	Y	U	E	I	X
M	A	G	I	C	Y	B	U	D	A
O	Y	E	F	Y	K	L	Z	D	P
N	O	S	E	E	N	E	M	Y	K
S	K	H	D	P	O	X	A	T	B
T	E	A	M	S	B	F	S	H	Y
E	A	R	I	A	U	K	K	M	E
R	E	P	O	W	E	R	S	Q	S

Planets
Teams
Masks
Giddy
Nerd
Super
Trust
Win
Yes

Powers
Enemy
Monster
Magic
S.O.S.
Secrets
Sharp
Super

Masks
Saw
Shy
Bud
Trouble
Wrong
Passwords
Shield

Captain Cosmic's Word Find #4

A	M	A	Z	I	N	G	Z	A	R
W	F	N	P	W	L	O	M	R	H
E	N	G	K	H	F	B	E	A	M
S	I	R	Y	C	U	L	R	C	G
O	S	Y	I	S	P	I	D	E	R
M	L	U	O	U	K	N	H	R	G
E	O	A	O	P	M	A	S	C	F
k	A	U	L	E	A	D	E	R	S
G	D	V	Y	R	X	O	T	D	S
C	A	P	G	V	F	A	S	O	H
O	D	A	T	I	U	G	O	M	E
M	I	A	L	L	S	R	C	E	Y
I	F	X	H	L	A	F	U	N	E
C	R	U	S	A	D	E	R	H	B
R	S	K	C	I	F	V	G	E	O
A	V	Q	U	N	D	H	E	R	O

Hero
Crusader
Urge
Comic
Spider
Angry
Sir

Smazing
Gun
Boo
All
Beam
Goblin
Spider

Awesome
Super Villain
Cap
Me
Racer
Leader

Cracking the Secret Code Word Find #5

C	O	M	P	R	O	M	I	S	E
O	P	S	O	N	T	E	M	A	N
O	Y	T	W	E	W	D	U	V	E
L	S	I	E	I	P	I	K	P	M
C	N	A	R	M	U	A	L	L	Y
A	M	N	E	Q	R	T	S	G	T
T	E	A	M	Y	G	O	O	P	G
U	A	S	U	X	U	R	G	R	S
A	N	T	I	N	B	U	S	O	I
G	P	I	C	V	L	I	F	T	T
I	S	W	T	Q	A	G	C	E	P
O	U	T	E	R	S	P	A	C	E
N	I	P	M	X	T	Y	N	T	C
C	G	A	P	W	O	D	D	S	I
W	A	S	E	N	F	Q	A	G	V
F	E	A	R	V	F	L	Y	E	R

Compromise	Flyer	Team
Outer Space	Gap	Odd
Temper	Protect	Goop
Blastoff	Anti	We
Arm	Mean	Cool Cat
Enemy	All	Mediator
Lift	Am	Power
Fear	Day	Ally

Swashbuckling Super Word Find #6

V	A	P	O	R	I	Z	E	D	J
I	U	O	F	A	K	I	V	A	T
C	J	S	X	D	L	Y	I	N	L
T	Y	I	U	I	P	F	L	Y	V
I	K	T	A	O	S	Z	K	I	S
M	A	I	J	A	J	Y	I	L	K
R	W	V	P	C	W	S	P	Y	U
U	C	F	W	I	T	N	E	S	S
R	Z	K	R	V	J	A	P	D	E
I	S	I	N	C	E	R	E	W	E
U	T	P	U	S	X	L	S	P	K
H	A	R	M	I	C	R	Y	I	I
I	L	S	D	U	I	J	E	W	C
D	K	W	I	K	T	I	L	A	D
K	D	Y	S	F	E	E	L	U	O
S	V	E	N	T	U	O	W	E	S

Feel
Do
Lad
Positive
Sonar
Excite
Evil
Yell

Cry
Witness
Sincere
Victim
Fly
Seek
Vat

Harm
Vaporize
Radioactive
Vent
Spy
Yes
Stalk

Adventures in Mad Libs #1

On an ordinary (adj.)________________________ day in (month) ________________________ ,
my villain (name), ________________________ woke up in a very (adj.) ____________ mood.
He was (adj) ________________________and feeling (adj)________________________.
He was out to cause (noun) ____________________with his villain suit on, he (verb) ______________
for his underground (noun) ________________________.

What is that old superhero (name) ________________________ doing today, he wondered.
If I (verb)________________________ maybe I'll find him and (verb) ________________.
He wants to make the (noun) ________________________ better and I want it all for myself.
I guess you could call me (adj.) ________________________.

Oh, there's (name) ____________________ now. I'll try using my new (noun) ________________
on him and see how it (verb) ____________________s. Look, he's (adj.) ________________!
He (verb) ________________________over to the fallen superhero who suddenly, faster than you
can (verb) ____________________, flew up into the air and (verb) ____________________
the villain on the (noun) ________________________.

Adventures in Mad Libs #2

One (adj.) ________________________ morning, my superhero (name) , ____________________
went to work at (place)____________________. He thought today was going to be a (adj.) ______________
day, but instead, it turned out to be very (adj.) ________________________.

In the big city the weather was (adj.)________________, and people were (adj.) ________________.
Suddenly, (name)________________________saw from the window by his desk, a man hanging from the
(noun)____________________. He knew he had to act (adverb) ________________________,
so he (verb) ________________________ (adverb) ________________, just in time before
the man (verb) ________________________ to the ground.

On the sidewalk, the city police were ready holding a large (noun) ________________________.
They were (adj.) ________________ relieved when they saw that (name) ____________________
rescued the dangling man. (name) ____________________ brought the man (adverb) ______________
to the ground where crowds of (noun) ____________________ cheered (adverb) ______________.
Once again, (name) ________________________saved the day in the big city!

Cosmic Kernels Found

Approximate Time: 10 minutes

Objective: To incorporate Science into the program.

Materials: about ¼ cup of popcorn kernels, a tall, clear jar, a cold carbonated clear soda.

Directions: Pour the chilled soda into the jar. Add the kernels and watch them sink to the bottom, swim to the top, and repeat the cycle. Now that we've discovered the cosmic kernels, what can we use them for? Have students brainstorm ways to use this experiment as a metaphor.

Recipe for Top Secret High Intensity Beams

Approximate Time: 10 minutes

Objective: To incorporate science into the program.

Materials: paper plates with a lip around the edge, milk, 4 colors of food coloring, liquid dish soap (any kind), and toothpicks.

Directions: Pour milk onto the plate until the bottom is barely covered. Drop one drop of each color of food coloring onto the plate, being careful to space them out. Dip the tip of the toothpick into the liquid soap and place the tip down in the center of the plate and watch the beams come to life. After a few minutes of experimenting, students may use the toothpicks to swirl the colors together. This creates a marbling effect.

Section 6: Relaxation & Guided Imagery

Approximate Time: 15 minutes for each exercise.

Objective: To provide time for relaxing and reflecting on the program and using guided imagery for self-empowerment.

Visualization can be the most empowering technique of all. Let's face it, there is so much crammed into the typical school day, it's no wonder students are restless, fidgety, agitated and prone to bad choices in behavior. Relaxation techniques or guided imagery can be a small safe haven in the day, a time when the mind is allowed to roam free and relaxation is encouraged. Many children are never read to outside of school, and most children find that being read to is very soothing.

These reflections are designed to supplement the Superheroes curriculum, and can be used either to start a session or at the end of a session. Either way, try to be consistent about when you use it so that children will begin to look forward to these sessions. Playing soft music in the background can help set the tone of peace and relaxation faster. If a child falls asleep, let him be. He will still benefit from the relaxation and can still hear the words on some level.

I Am My Own Superhero – Self-Confidence

Close your eyes. Be sure you are sitting or lying down in a comfortable position. Be aware of your breathing as you slowly breathe in and out. The air you inhale will energize you, the air you exhale will relax you. Concentrate on breathing slowly and deeply for a minute. Sit still and think about all your good traits. The ones that make you who you are, the ones people love you for…Now think about the superhero you created. Picture him or her in your mind…think about the great qualities you gave your superhero…. and the very special superpower you endowed him with…think about whether or not your positive traits are similar to those you gave your superhero…Is your character more like you or less like you?…Continue concentrating on your breathing….now imagine what it would feel like to own the superpower you gave your character. What things would you be able to do that you can't do now? How would you use your superpower? Would it help you create conflict or peace? Would the world be a better place because of it? Think about what you as a superhero believe in….what do you stick up for? How do you help people? Have you been a responsible superhero?

Now go back to thinking about your own positive traits. Think about them carefully...do you think there is a superhero inside you? Maybe you can't fly or leap tall buildings, but there are lots of things you can do to let the superhero inside you out…to make the world a better place….to help people, or animals, or the environment…..picture yourself doing some of these things…take your time and continue to focus on your breathing…continue relaxing as you think of the ways in which you are a superhero...and say to yourself: I am my own superhero. I am my own superhero.

Now slowly begin to open your eyes, wiggle your fingers and toes, and stretch….and now let's talk about this experience.

The Shining Star – Relaxation

Close your eyes, lie down comfortably or put your head on your desk, and breath slowly, concentrating on your breath. Lie perfectly still and imagine that you are standing in a field of tall grass and it is dark out. The dark sky is clear, and you can see hundreds of shining, twinkling stars….Many of the stars are winking at you as you lie relaxed and breathing slowly…. the stars shimmer in the night sky like sparkling diamonds… there is a happy star, a silly star, a love star, a shy star, a peace star. It is the most beautiful night sky you have ever seen. You lie there comfortable, relaxed and feeling safe. The happy star fills you with happy thoughts….the love star reminds you to love yourself and those around you, and the peace star reminds you that there can be peace inside yourself and in the real world if we only try to solve conflicts in a peaceful way….. are there any other kinds of stars you see up in that dark sky? Enjoy looking at the glittery stars, the way they form patterns in the sky, the way they make you feel. Keep being aware of your slow breathing.

Now slowly begin to open your eyes, wiggle your fingers and toes, slowly let daylight into your eyes. Let's talk about this experience.

I am my own Superhero: Self-Empowerment

Close your eyes, lie down comfortably or put your head on your desk…breathe slowly, concentrating on your breath flowing in and out of your body. Imagine that you are a Superhero. You are wearing a superhero costume, and you have your own special superpowers. You put your arms up in the air and suddenly you are gliding, up over the tops of buildings and roads, soaring higher and higher. You realize how free you feel as you fly around your city or town. Picture yourself looking down at everyone and knowing when you see someone in trouble. Imagine how good you feel inside knowing you can help those in trouble…where do you feel that good feeling inside yourself? Now, slowly picture yourself coming back to the ground, to the earth, and try to hold onto that good feeling inside as you slowly open your eyes and look around you. Let's talk about this experience.

The Cat and the Bird – Conflict Resolution

Close your eyes, lie down comfortably or put your head on your desk...breathe slowly, concentrating on your breath flowing in and out of your body. Imagine that you are in a canoe on a lake, and you are in the middle of the canoe paddling. On one end of the canoe is an orangey colored cat, and on the other end is a beautiful little brown bird. You are in between them…..you are relaxed as you paddle, feeling happy because it's such a beautiful day and the sun is shining brightly….suddenly you realize that the cat is hungry. She is licking her lips and beginning to move around. The little bird is just enjoying the ride. Oh no, you think, the cat might eat the bird! What can I do to stop that from happening? How can I get them to be friends rather than enemies? The bird could fly over to the cat and peck him. I'm realizing they don't like each other very much at all…what can I do to help them find some way to agree and not hate each other?

Thinking back on what I learned about resolving conflicts, I realize I am my own superhero, and that I may indeed be able to stop the cat and the bird from hurting each other. I begin talking to them both, trying to point out all they have in common – they're both afraid, they both want to survive, they are both stuck on a canoe (although the bird can fly, he cannot fly as far away as the shoreline). At first I feel frustrated. Neither one seems to understand the other's point of view. I understand both points of view, so I continue to mediate a discussion between the cat and the bird. Gradually, the bird realizes that he has no reason to attack the cat if the cat leaves him alone. He starts to feel relieved. The cat gradually begins to understand that the bird isn't going to attack him, and that if he's hungry he can ask me to catch a fish for him. He'd much prefer that anyway. Before long, the bird is sitting on the cat's back, and they have become friends. I am feeling very happy and relieved – I am a superhero and I fulfilled this mission to everyone's advantage. Everyone wins with this solution. I was able to resolve this mission peacefully. I'll take a deep breath and pat myself on the back.

Slowly open your eyes and let the daylight in. Stretch and wiggle your fingers and toes. Now let's sit in a circle and discuss this experience.

Teambuilding – the Joining of Hands

Close your eyes, lie down comfortably or put your head on your desk…breathe slowly concentrating on your breath flowing in and out of your body. Feel yourself relax, first in your feet and toes, then in your legs, your belly, your arms, your face. Breathe slowly remaining aware of your breath going in and out of yourself.

When you feel relaxed, picture yourself as part of a group who is standing in a circle. Inside the circle is the earth, with its vast blue oceans, and deep green forests, the yellow lights of the city, and the white of the polar caps. You are part of a special group of kids who are holding hands in a circle looking at the earth and all its precious resources. Each of you is a superhero. You feel the hand of the friend on either side of you. You are smiling at the friends on the other side of the earth. They are smiling back at you. Everyone is happy and relaxed. You are wondering why it is this way. Then you realize that you are a special person with unique superpowers who is part of a team, each of whom are also special in different ways. Each of you looks different, acts different and dresses differently than the others and yet you all belong to this thing called a team. It's a lot like the Justice League.

A team is a group of people who work together toward a common goal. It could be something small like keeping your classroom neat and clean, or something huge, like helping to save the environment. Whatever it is, you will be asked to add your ideas and skills to the project. If everyone adds their unique self to the project, everyone is sure to win.

As you continue to breathe slowly, think about what it is that makes you unique and special. Is it your sense of humor? Is it your ability to run fast or play music? Could it be that you are smart in a subject many others struggle in? Could it be that you are a considerate person, a good friend and a good citizen?

As you are feeling relaxed, think about that special or unique thing you bring to the group as you again picture everyone holding hands with the earth in the middle. The group has agreed on a goal and one by one each superhero adds their specialness to the project. When it's your turn, you try your hardest to help, using your special superpowers and strengths, and finally when everyone has done their part, the whole group is holding up the earth, each person holding equal weight. There you stand as a team, arms up in the air and the earth spins as you walk around slowly in a circle. Everyone is smiling because everyone has worked together, and everyone wins!

Slowly open your eyes and let the daylight in. Stretch and wiggle your fingers and toes. Now let's sit in a circle and discuss this experience.

Anger Diffuser

Close your eyes, lie down comfortably or put your head on your desk…breathe slowly concentrating on your breath flowing in and out of your body. You are feeling angry. Your muscles are tight and tense. Your face is tight and puckered. Your fists are clenched and you are crying. Your mind is racing and you keep thinking about the thing that made you feel so angry. It's just not fair, you say to yourself. How dare something or someone not take my feelings seriously. It just makes me so so angry.

Then you suddenly remember the S.U.P.E.R. phrase you just learned. The S stands for "stop." Stop and think about the situation. Notice your breath as it goes in and out of you. Try breathing deeply, the kind of breathing where you take a slow deep breath. Your belly goes up as you breathe in, and goes down as you breathe out. Stay focused on breathing slowly and deeply. We call this ballooning. As you use balloon breaths slowly, try to think about relaxing yourself from your head right down to your toes. Let's start with your head. Let go of your facial tension. Feel your face relax as you use balloon breaths slowly. Once you feel your face relax, try feeling your shoulders and neck become relaxed. Let that relaxed feeling float slowly and gently down your arms until it reaches the tips of your fingers.

Now you remember that the "u" in S.U.P.E.R. stands for understanding the situation. Try to understand what made you angry and what made someone else angry. Continue to breathe deeply and slowly. Feel how much better your head and upper body feels since your muscles relaxed. Try to feel your belly relax as you take slow balloon breaths. Feel the angry feelings slowly disappear as you let your breath out. Try picturing a dragon who breathes fire. It's anger comes out into the open as he exhales. What does it feel like to you? Does the fire turn into vapor as the dragon lets it out? Is he feeling better inside?

The "p" in S.U.P.E.R. stands for placing yourself in the other person's shoes. Try to feel your legs relax as you use balloon breaths. Keep breathing in and out slowly, while you let that relaxed feeling sink to your ankles, and then your toes. Finally the tips of your toes are relaxed and you can breathe while feeling yourself relaxed from your head to your toes. Try to picture yourself as the other person, and think as you breathe slowly, how that person might be feeling. Do you think the feelings might be similar to yours? Do you think they are different from yours? What does it feel like to be in that other person's shoes? Keep breathing balloon breaths slowly as you think this all through.

The "e" in S.U.P.E.R. stands for encouraging other ideas or alternatives. Is there anything about your situation that could have been done differently? Are there any other possible solutions you can think of? Continue breathing slowly in and out as you think about this. Is there anything you would change if you could go back and redo the situation? Would you act differently? If you acted differently, do you think that would cause the other person to act differently?

As you continue your balloon breaths, you are remembering that the "r" in S.U.P.E.R. stands for responding appropriately. Is there anything you would like to say to the other person now that you are feeling more relaxed? Is there anything you want the other person to say to you? Are you feeling ready to put the situation into the past? Continue breathing for a few more minutes. When you are ready, open your eyes slowly. When you are ready, let's talk about this experience.

- **S** Slow Down
- **U** Understand the situation
- **P** Place yourself in the other's shoes
- **E** Encourage other ideas
- **R** Respond appropriately

Section 7 –The Psychology of Superheroes

In American culture, commercial superheroes have many important qualities in common. They have alien origins, have experienced trauma at a very early age – often violently, and grow up without their birth parents in an altered type of nuclear family. And they have all survived and ultimately rose above their misfortunes. Virtually all superheroes strive to improve themselves, hone in on their skills and superpowers, and that striving is a quest.

Many superheroes have dual or secret identities. This quality assists them in rising above their obstacles, helps them express their most basic longings and needs, and fosters an integration of polar opposites in their nature as a superhero, and as a human being.

As an archetype, the superhero has had staying power for decades because we need them on many psychological levels. We all need positive role model heroes to look up to. People from most cultures can relate to a superhero. The fact that they aren't real is all the more reason for admiration, as they are a step removed from our daily lives.

> Indick (2004) states:
> As the central figure in the film experience, the hero is the integral archetype in the collective unconscious of American culture. He is at once a collective and personal encounter, as each individual in the audience identifies personally with the hero's story, while the hero simultaneously embodies the collective hopes and ideals of the culture that creates him. It is this compound phenomenon – the personal identification with the collective hero – that makes the hero archetype so psychologically powerful. This compound identification with the hero fulfills what Carl Jung called the "transcendent function" of myth and dreams.

Superman™ is a good example of a superhero who has changed and evolved over the years according to changes in society's needs and wants. Each new generation will continue to mold him according to the needs of their time because some ideas are universal and eternal. He embodies the values of "Truth, Justice and the American Way," transcending and bridging each generation into the next one, carrying those ideas and ideals with him, giving them a living form to which we can relate within the context of our own historical moments. At the same time as a function of both the social collective and personal motivation, Superman™ clearly established that with great power also comes great responsibility. And at that most personal of levels, through superheroes, of which Superman™ is one, we come to feel things will be ok, if we just have faith in our abilities and ourselves. This is powerful and affecting stuff, indeed.

Jung and Archetypes

Psychologist C. G. Jung coined the phrase Collective Unconscious. This is a collection of memories and types of characters called archetypes, which all of mankind are assumed to share. The collective unconscious is a group ideal, whereas each of us has our own individual unconscious.

Carl Jung developed his theory on the collective unconscious after a series of dreams in the fall of 1913. Jung first began dreaming of floods covering the earth that later turned to blood and cold winters. At first he thought himself becoming psychotic until August of the following year World War I broke out and he began to see a connection between himself as an individual and humanity in general.

A self-taught expert on ancient religions, myths, and stories (he could even read in the original Sanskrit language of Hinduism) Jung began to look at the commonalities among various societies and determined there are "mystical collective ideas" among mankind in general. According to Jung (1959) the collective unconscious goes beyond personal experience to a deeper layer and is: "identical in all men, and thus constitutes a common psychic substrate of a supra-personal nature which is present in every one of us."

Jung believed myths are "the first and foremost psychic phenomena that reveal the nature of the soul" (p.359). Similar to Freud's instinct archetypes are an "organizing principle" of our actions and defined by Jung as: "typical forms of behavior which, once they become conscious, naturally present themselves as ideas and images like everything else that becomes a content of consciousness (p.123)". Differing from Freud's instincts Jung did not see these behaviors as biological but more as spiritual in nature.

Jung began to analyze his, and other peoples dreams and discovered common characters that exemplified specific behaviors. For the purpose of this book we will examine four of these behaviors, or archetypes: the Anima, the Animus, the Persona, and the Shadow.

The Shadow comes from our most base instincts and is concerned with basic survival and reproduction. If Jung were alive today he would probably place the Shadow as surviving on the first rung of Maslow's Hierarchy of Needs and provide the basis for our knowledge of the "Primitive brain," and what Daniel Goleman(1995) termed, based on Joseph LeDoux's research, an "Amygdala Hijacking". The shadow is the evil we are all capable of performing. Think of Darth Vadar and the "dark side" of a Jedi Knight being the place we store our Shadow. As we refer to bullying behavior as an evil action, instead of seeing the "Bully" as an evil person, we need to see that the Shadow is the bullying side of the individual. Our pets are capable of showing their off-spring incredible love and then vicious killing to provide food in a very short amount of time. Our pets are amoral, yet we may see their actions as base, primitive, or even evil.

The Persona is the image we all project to the public. Think of the mask we put on for the outside world every day. It begins as the impression we want others to see when we go out into the world. The Persona protects our deeper selves. Sometimes we feel safe when we present a happy-go-lucky persona to the world even though we are feeling extremely vulnerable to the world. Sometimes we present an opposite "tough-guy" persona to the world even though we are feeling equally vulnerable. We use the Persona to manipulate people's opinions and behaviors. At times others mistake the Persona for the true self, and sometimes we even convince ourselves that this mask is our true image.

The final two Archetypes we want to discuss are the Anima and Animus. These are the male and female roles we play in our daily lives. For most of us this role is determined by our gender and the behaviors society says are appropriate for that role. Freud, Jung, Adler, Erikson, and other leading fathers of Psychology saw this role as more fluid in nature. Society blurs these roles more today, yet we still hold on to historic images of these roles; i.e. Davy Crockett, Polly Purebred, and the Marlboro Man are all gender specific roles assigned from our own collective folklore in the United States. Jung felt focusing on only one gender role limited our growth potential and so encouraged an exploration of both sides believing a fully developed balance is our healthiest self. As the terms Metro sexual and Emo continue to grow among our youth today these lines are blurring a little more. There is not enough research to show if this is truly healthy and what Jung and others were visualizing.

The Anima is the female side present in our collective unconscious of men and the Animus is the male side present in females. Jung's anima was a young girl. Other men may see her as a sweet witch. She is usually the spontaneous and intuitive aspect of our personality most likely being the most emotional part. The Animus is the wise old man side, Yoda or Merlin, and is the most logical part. It is also the aggressive, argumentative aspect of our personality.

Staying with the Star Wars examples you can see how Princess Leia began as the vulnerable young princess seeking help from her hero. As the story progresses we see a stronger leader emerge. This is Leia's Animus emerging and completing the whole to communicate effectively with the collective unconscious. Luke and Hans begin their journey as tough talking guys who begin to show a more sensitive and caring side as the story progresses.

The Myers- Briggs Type Indicator (MBTI) is a way of looking at Jung's Archetypes to demonstrate how different parts of our collective unconscious are stronger than others, yet combined demonstrates what behaviors make up our personality. It is important to note there are no rights and wrongs in the Archetypes or in Myers – Briggs. It is not a way of defining the person. It is merely a way to understand behavior, how we all have these behaviors in common throughout human existence, and most importantly for Jung to find a balance.

Adlerian Perspective

From the perspective of Adlerian theory, behavior is goal-oriented. The primary goal of Adlerian therapy is to help the client move from misbehavior to healthy goals and behaviors. Psychologist Rudolf Dreikurs (1964) identified four primary motivations for children's misbehavior:

- Attention
- Power
- Revenge
- Proving inadequacy

Psychologists Dinkmeyer and McKay (1989) identified four goals that motivate children to have positive behaviors:

- Attention, involvement and contribution
- Autonomy and Self-responsibility
- Justice and fairness
- The avoidance of conflict and acceptance of other's opinions.

Classic Adlerian therapy is made up of four distinct phases. Phase one involves establishing a therapeutic relationship, unconditional acceptance, mutual trust, honesty and understanding. This relationship becomes the steppingstone for all that follows in the progression of therapy. Phase two in Adlerian therapy involves exploring the client's lifestyle, history, goals, self-image, social interactions, and feelings. The third phase involves helping the client gain insight into his or her lifestyle, reaction patterns, feelings, self-image, and relationships. At this stage, role playing superheroes and discussing their perceived powers can be very helpful. Stage four in Adlerian therapy is used to help the client learn and practice a new self-image, new behaviors, and new ways of dealing with feelings. It can be helpful in this stage for children to keep a superhero in mind so that they can quickly think, "What would Superman™ do," for example, when confronted with an unsettling situation.

When children are given a choice of role-playing a superhero or a villain and they choose the villain, we have found it beneficial to work with that choice. Usually those children have chosen the negative role because that is how they think others perceive them. They are used to being identified as the "bad guy." It is akin to being the identified patient in a dysfunctional family. Once comfortable in the villain's role, a child can usually be convinced to try the superhero role. If a child refuses, the virtues of the villain can be explored. In the exercise section of this book, you will see ways to help children begin to change their self-image and negative behaviors by identifying with the superhero of their choice.

The Gestalt Perspective

A gestalt is a pattern or configuration, of which the whole is greater than the sum of its parts. Because of its emphasis on holism, gestalt therapy assumes the inseparability of mind, body, emotions, and spirituality. Therefore, if a child has an emotional disturbance, it will be experienced as a psychological and a physiological experience. Gestalt therapy tends to attract practitioners and clients who are interested in a very experiential approach.

Our brains are always looking to connect ideas to form patterns in order to create meaning in them. The main goal of Gestalt therapy is to enable the individual to achieve homeostasis, or the ability to remain balanced under a variety of life circumstances. Because of the emphasis on holism, Gestalt therapy is particularly well suited to integrating the right and left hemispheres of the brain. As in other developmental theories, one stage needs to be mastered before moving on to a new stage. Changing situations give rise to the individual feeling discomfort. Feeling discomfort prompts the individual to find new solutions so they can grow.

Although psychologists disagree on the number of stages in Gestalt therapy, the stages, like the developmental theories, overlap. Gestalt play therapy helps create awareness of a child's emotions and begins to teach them how to satisfy that emotion in a positive light.

Blom (2004) has outlined five stages in Gestalt play therapy. In stage one, called the Awareness/Sensation stage, the individual experiences a need or is disturbed by an environmental stimulus…becomes aware of it, assigns meaning to it and experiences specific emotions related to it. In stage two, the Mobilization/Choice of Relevant Action stage, the awareness of a need is followed by a mobilization of the self and resources in order to satisfy the need. The healthy person is now ready for choosing a course of action. Stage Three, the Final Contact/Action stage sees the individual become fully involved in the course of action chosen to satisfy his or her need. In stage four, the Post-Contact stage, once contact has been completed, the child experiences homeostasis. The final stage five involves withdrawal. The person withdraws to a state of rest or equilibrium between the destruction of one gestalt and the formation of a new gestalt (need).

Gestalt techniques are well suited to superhero play for many reasons. They help children discover the polarities within themselves. Superheroes exhibit polarities just by virtue of their double personas. One of the main objectives of the Gestalt approach is the natural therapeutic progression or integration. Integration helps us to incorporate our emotions, cognition, physical sensations, and spirituality. By role-playing and learning to look at superheroes as positive role models, children are experientially trying these roles on for size in an accepting environment. In so doing, they become aware of and process the polarities within themselves, thus achieving a more balanced sense of self.

In as yet another aspect, superpowers include flight, speed, invulnerability, acute sensory capacity, invisibility, and genius. Conversely, each of the famous superheroes also has an inherent weakness, or vulnerability, which imposes a limit on them, and in certain ways, makes them more human and less superhuman. For example, Superman's nemesis is kryptonite. Whenever he comes into contact with the substance, he fears for his life.

Superheroes exhibit polarities just by virtue of their double personas. Integration is one of the main objectives of Gestalt techniques. Integration helps us to integrate our emotions, cognition, physical sensations, and spirituality. By role-playing and learning to look at superheroes as positive role models, children are experientially trying these roles on for size in an accepting environment.

Web Sites for Emotional Literacy, Peace, and Social Justice*

Below are web sites that relate to this program in some way. This list is by no means exhaustive; these are web sites we came into contact with while putting this program together. We suggest a class site-finding activity.

www.amnestyusa.org – Amnesty International

www.blackseek.com – about Black history, heroes and heroines

www.centerforsafeschools.org. The Center for Safe Schools.

www.comicvine.com/characters - Comic Vine information on superheroes

www.epals.com – E-pals for connecting classrooms to each other through email

www.esrnational.org – Educators for Social Responsibility

www.facinghistory.org - Facing History and Ourselves

www.fau.edu/library/brodytoc.htm - Jewish history and culture.

www.haguepeace.org – The Hague Appeal for Peace

www.internationalhero.co.uk – Information about international superheroes

www.myhero.com – Information on heroes

www.ncpc.org. The National Crime Prevention Council On-Line Resource Center.

www.peacecorps.gov/wws/ - The United States Peace Corp

www.peacegames.org – Peace Games organization

www.peaceheroes.com – put together by volunteers for a better future.

www.pa.org – Project Adventure

www.stopbullyingnow.hrsa.gov – Bullying Information from the government

www.teachablemoment.org – Teachable Moment organization

www.teachingforchange.org – Teaching for Change organization

www.teachingtolerance.org – A Project of Southern Poverty Law Center

www.t4sj.org – Teacher for Social Justice

www.tolerance.org – A Project of Southern Poverty Law Center

www.wagingpeace.org – about working toward peace

www.womeninworldhistory.org - about female heroines

www.un.org – United Nations Web Site – Cyber School Bus

www.usip.org/ - The United States Institute of Peace

* As of the time this book went to press, each of these web sites were fully active.

Resources

The Super Student Program by Dr. John Chanaca, is a wonderful resource for all who work with students in grades K-5. It contains a comprehensive, multi-faceted, multi-media program with school success stories and focus skills activities and a survival kit for teachers and parents. The Super Student Program was designed to improve student achievement and behavior by using positive reinforcement, personal responsibility and teaching student the survival skills necessary to believe in themselves as winners. Super Student is available through www.youthlightbooks.com

Dick Blick Art Materials
www.dickblick.com

Folkmanis Puppets
www.folkkmanis.com

Lakeshore Learning Materials
www.lakeshorelearning.com

Magic Cabin
www.magiccabin.com

Pearl Art Supplies
www.pearlpaint.com

Triarco Art Supplies
www.triarcoarts.com

References

American Art Therapy Association (2008). www.arttherapy.org.

Blom, R. (2006). The handbook of gestalt play therapy. Philadelphia: Jessica Kingsley Publishers.

Campbell, J. (1988). *The power of myth.* New York: Doubleday.

Erikson, E. (1980). *Identity and the life cycle.* New York: Norton.

Goleman, D. (2005). *Emotional intelligence.* New York: Bantam Books.

Gardner, H. (1993). *Frames of mind: the theory of multiple intelligences.* New York: Basic Books.

Hoffman, E. (2004). *Magic capes, amazing powers: transforming superhero play in the classroom.* St. Paul: Redleaf Press.

Indick, W. (November 18, 2004) *Classical heroes in modern movies: mythological patterns of the superhero.* Journal of Media Psychology. Vol. 9, No. 3.

Johnson, S. (2004). *Mind wide open.* New York: Scribner.

Jung, C. G. (1993). T*he basic writings of C.G. Jung.* New York: Modern Library.

Kotulak, R. (1996). *Inside the brain.* Kansas City: Andrews McMeel.

Kreidler, W. and Furlong, L. (1986). *Adventures in peacemaking: A conflict resolution activity guide for school-age programs.* Cambridge, MA: Educators for Social Responsibility.

Kreidler, W. (1984). *Creative conflict resolution.* Glenview, IL: Scott, Foresman and Company.

Lawrence, J. S. and Jewett, R. (2002) *The myth of the american superhero.* Grand Rapids, MI: William B. Eerdmans Publishing Company.

LeDoux, J. (2002). *Synaptic self.* New York: Penguin Books.

Liebmann, M. (1986). *Art therapy for groups.* Cambridge, MA: Brookline Books.

Lowenfeld, V., and Brittain, W. (1987). *Creative and mental growth,* 8th Edition. Upper Saddle River, NJ: Prentice Hall, Inc.

May, R. (1991). *The cry for myth.* New York: W.W. Norton & Company.

Paley, V. (2004). *A child's work: the importance of fantasy play.* Chicago: University Of Chicago Press.

Reynolds, R. (1994) *Superheroes: A Modern Mythology.* Jackson, MS: University of Mississippi Press.

Rubin, L. C., Editor. (2007). *Using superheroes in counseling and play therapy.* New York: Springer Publishing Company.

Schrumpf, F., Crawford, D., and Bodine, R. (1997). *Peer mediation, conflict resolution in schools - student manual.* Champaign, IL: Research Press.

Sendak, M. (1963). *Where the wild things are.* New York: Harper/Trophy.

Singer, D., and Revenson, T. (1996). *A Piaget Primer: How a child thinks.* New York: Penguin Books.

Winner, E. (1982). *Invented Worlds, the Psychology of the Arts*. Cambridge, MA: Harvard University Press.

Recommended Resources

Adler, R. & Towne, N. (1999). *Looking Out, Looking In,* 9th Edition. New York: Harcourt Brace.

Andreasen, N. C. (2006). *The creative brain.* New York: Penguin Group.

Beane, A. (1999). *The bully free classroom.* Minneapolis: Free Spirit Press. Therapeutics.

Bodine, R., Crawford, D., Schrumpf, F. (2002). *Creating the peaceable school: A Comprehensive Program for Teaching Conflict Resolution.* Champaign, IL: Research Press.

Chanaca, J. (2005). *The super student program.* Chapin, SC: Youthlight Publishing.

Dyson, A. H. (1997). *Writing Superheroes.* New York: Teacher's College Press.

Fingeroth, D. (2004). *Superman on the Couch.* New York: Continuum.

Kohl, M. F. (1999). *Making make-believe.* Beltsville, MD: Gryphon House.

LeDoux, J. (1996). *The emotional brain.* New York: Simon & Schuster.

Lowenstein, L. (1999). *Creative interventions for troubled children & youth.* Toronto: Champion Press.

Scearce, C. (1992). *100 Ways to build teams.* Palatine, Ill: Skylight Publishing.

Simmonds, J. (2003). *Seeing red: an anger management and peacemaking curriculum for kids.* Canada: New Society Publishers.

Vernon, A. (1989). *Thinking, feeling, behaving: an emotional education curriculum for adolescents.* Champaign, Ill: Research Press.

Wood, C. (1994). *Yardsticks – children in the classroom Ages 4-14.* Greenfield, MA: Northeast Foundation for Children.

Facilitator's Questionnaire

Superheroes Unmasked was created from careful research and years of experience working with students of all ages teaching emotional literacy. We take our commitment to this task very seriously, and would greatly value your input as a facilitator. Your responses will enable us to understand what you found helpful, as well as what suggestions you have.

All responses will be kept confidential; signing or tagging with identifiable school information is optional. We very much appreciate your efforts in this important facet of children's education.

School or location name: ______________________________

Address ______________________________

Telephone number______________________

Grades or ages of children in this program______________________

Facilitator's background______________________

Years of experience in position______________________

Superheroes Unmasked was implemented (circle one)

during regular school hours

after school

in a separate setting

Number of children in each session______________________

Was the emotional content of this program new to these children? Yes/No

Did children grasp these concepts easily? Yes/No

Were there any lessons that you felt were too difficult? ______________________

Do you feel that the approach of using superheroes made it easier for children to grasp these difficult concepts? Yes/No

To what extent were your children's social attitudes and skills affected by the *Superheroes Unmasked* program? (One is the least affected, 10 is the maximum affected).

· Enthusiasm/happiness	1	2	3	4	5	6	7	8	9	10
· Openness and trust of others	1	2	3	4	5	6	7	8	9	10
· Tolerance/Acceptance of others	1	2	3	4	5	6	7	8	9	10
· Sensitivity, compassion, empathy	1	2	3	4	5	6	7	8	9	10
· Respect for others	1	2	3	4	5	6	7	8	9	10
· General attitude and behavior	1	2	3	4	5	6	7	8	9	10
· Increase of Self-Esteem	1	2	3	4	5	6	7	8	9	10
· Knowledge of conflict resolution	1	2	3	4	5	6	7	8	9	10

Comments/Suggestions______________________________

____

How were the following behaviors affected by the program? (1 is the least effect, 10 is the maximum).

· Opening up of closed cliques?	1 2 3 4 5 6 7 8 9 10
· Withdrawing, self isolation?	1 2 3 4 5 6 7 8 9 10
· Aggressive behavior (hostility, hitting, kicking, spitting, yelling, etc).	1 2 3 4 5 6 7 8 9 10
· Bullying (name calling, put downs, dissing, teasing, ostracizing)	1 2 3 4 5 6 7 8 9 10

Which type of children do you think benefited the most from this program?

· Children who have been bullied, teased or are loners

· Children who are bullies

· Children with exceptional leadership abilities

· Children with advanced artistic or musical abilities

· Children who are good athletes

How was children's academic performance indicators affected?

· Academic involvement and performance? ____________________

· Level of participation and attention span? ____________________

· Test scores and grades? ____________________

